KU-246-559

About this book *4*

best *49–60*

Parks & Beaches *50–51*
Eastside Museums *52*
Public Art *53*
Architecture *54*
Neighbourhoods *55*

Active Pursuits *56–57*
What's Free & Nearly Free *58*
Free Events *59*
For Children *60*

where to... *61–86*

EAT

Northwest Classics &
   American Cuisine *62–63*
Seafood & Vegetarian *64–65*
Asian & Sushi Cuisine *66*
Mexican/Nuevo-Latino *67*
Romantic/Bistro Dining *68*
Coffee Shops &
   Breakfast Bests *69*

SHOP

Men's and Women's
   Clothing *70–72*
Art & Antiques *73*
Books, CD's & Tapes *74*
Gifts *75*

Speciality Shops *76*
Kitsch, Funk & Retro *77*

BE ENTERTAINED

Theatre & Film *78*
Classical Music, Dance &
   Opera *79*
Rock, Jazz & Blues Venues *80*
Other Venues & Hang-outs *81*
Bars, Pubs & Taverns *82*
Spectator Sports Venues *83*

STAY

Luxury Hotels *84*
Mid-Range Hotels *85*
Budget Accommodation *86*

travel facts *87–93*

Arriving & Departing *88–89*
Essential Facts *88–91*
Public Transport *91–92*

Media & Communications *92–93*
Emergencies *93*

Credits, Acknowledgements and Titles in this Series *96*

About this book

CityPack Seattle is divided into six sections to cover the six most important aspects of your visit to Seattle. It includes:
- An overview of the city and its people
- Itineraries, walks and excursions
- The top 25 sights to visit
- What makes the city special
- Restaurants, hotels, shops and nightlife
- Practical information

In addition, easy-to-read side panels provide extra facts and snippets, highlights of places to visit and invaluable practical advice.

CROSS-REFERENCES

To help you make the most of your visit, cross-references, indicated by ➤ , show you where to find additional information about a place or subject.

MAPS

The fold-out map accompanying this book is a comprehensive street plan of Seattle.The first (or only) map reference given for each attraction refers to this map.
The Top 25 locator maps found on the inside front and back covers of the book itself are for quick reference. They show the top 25 sights, described on pages 24–48, which are clearly plotted by number (**1**–**25**, not page number) across the city. The second map reference given for the Top 25 sights refers to this map.

ADMISSION CHARGES

An indication of the admission charge (for all attractions) is given by categorising the standard adult rate as follows:
✋ Inexpensive (up to $5), moderate ($5–9) and expensive ($10 or more).

Top 25 locator map
(continues on inside
back cover)
◄

CityPack
Seattle

SUZANNE TEDESKO

Suzanne Tedesko has lived in Seattle since 1975. Having travelled all over the world, she has written travel books on a range of subjects. She has also worked as an urban ethnographer and as a producer for film, television and radio.

AA Publishing
Find out more about AA Publishing and the wide range of services the AA provides by visiting our website at *www.theAA.com*

Contents

life 5–12

Introducing Seattle 6–8
Seattle in Figures 9
A Chronology 10–11

People & Events
    from History 12

how to organise your time 13–22

Itineraries 14–15
Walks 16–17
Evening Strolls 18

Organised Sightseeing 19
Excursions 20–21
What's On 22

top 25 sights 23–48

1 Discovery Park 24
2 Alki Beach 25
3 The Hiram M. Chittenden
    Locks 26
4 Fishermen's Terminal 27
5 Woodland Park Zoo 28
6 Pacific Science Center 29
7 Space Needle 30
8 Experience Music Project 31
9 The Waterfront & Aquarium 32
10 Pike Place Market 33
11 Ferry to Bainbridge Island 34
12 Monorail to Seattle Center 35
13 Seattle Art Museum 36
14 Lake Union 37
15 Downtown 38
16 Pioneer Square 39

17 REI (Recreational
    Equipment Inc) 40
18 The International District 41
19 Volunteer Park 42
20 Museum of Flight 43
21 University of Washington 44
22 Henry Art Museum 45
23 Burke Museum of Natural
    History and Culture 46
24 Washington Park
    Arboretum 47
25 The Boeing Tour 48

Index 94–95

SEATTLE
life

Introducing Seattle *6–8*

Seattle in Figures *9*

A Chronology *10–11*

People & Events from History *12*

Introducing Seattle

Seattle brings to mind mountains and Microsoft, aeroplanes and espresso, stunning scenery and the 'Seattle sound'. Then there's water – everywhere you look – in freshwater lakes, canals, Puget Sound (pronounced 'PEW-jet') and the drizzle that optimists like to call 'liquid sunshine'.

Outdoor enthusiasts flock to the region's lush forests, mountains and waterways. Wilderness areas are easily accessible. The Cascade Mountains rise to the east, dominated by snow-capped volcanoes: Mt Baker, Glacier Peak and grandest of all, 14,410-foot Mt Rainier. To the west lie the rugged Olympic Mountains.

If the flavour of Seattle is the mocha of its excellent cafés, its colours are grey and green. As if unable to make up its mind, the city can be dark and gloomy in the morning and sparkling by afternoon. Or vice versa. And when Seattle sparkles, as it normally does in the summer, life doesn't get much better. With the first indication of spring, residents get giddy: Frisbees are resurrected and sunglasses unearthed as people head to the park or potter in their gardens.

Over the years, the Seattle area has produced a number of firsts in fields ranging from aerospace to outdoor adventure. At one time, references to Seattle as a company town acknowledged the pre-eminent position of the Boeing Company. Over the past decade, however, the emphasis has shifted considerably. Today, Seattle's work culture reflects the influences of software giant Microsoft and other high-tech companies – many located on the burgeoning Eastside.

The city has also become a major player in biotechnology, medical research and education. The Fred Hutchinson Cancer Research Center performs more bone marrow transplants than anywhere else in the country while the University of Washington's School of Medicine receives major research grants, and its family practice training is ranked tops in the nation.

In 1989 Seattle was voted the nation's 'most livable city'. The thriving economy of the Clinton presidency and an influx of high-tech companies infused the region with wealth. New office towers competed for airspace while cultural institutions like museums and theatres moved into dazzling new homes or substantially remodelled old ones. Voters passed initiatives to tear down the maligned Kingdome and build two elaborate new sports stadiums – Safeco Field, home of the Mariners baseball team, and a new stadium for the Seahawks, Seattle's professional football team. Seattle seemed to have it all: natural beauty, jobs, cultural amenities – plus the relaxed lifestyle of a smaller town. The people came: between 1980 and 1990, the city's population grew by nearly 20 per cent.

As the millennium neared its close, Seattle was becoming a victim of its own success. New surveys indicated Seattle's traffic now ranked third worst in the nation and housing prices had risen well above the national average. Detractors charged that Seattle's priorities were misplaced: that this once egalitarian city was losing its soul.

In November 1999, an unlikely event shook Seattle. The World Trade Organisation (WTO) scheduled its international conference for Seattle. Despite prior warnings, city government failed to adequately prepare for the massive demonstrations. Although many citizens just engaged in peaceful protest, the media focused on the violent acts of a few and the intemperate response of police. Many locals were shocked and humbled by what they saw. Seattle was a small town no more.

In February 2001, an earthquake measuring 6.8 on the Richter scale rocked Seattle. Although damage was minimal, the event further shook Seattle's confidence. Just days later, Boeing

THE INVISIBLE THRONG

A famous speech by Chief Sealth reminds us of the Seattle area's original inhabitants: 'And when the last Red Man shall have perished...these shores will swarm with the invisible dead of my tribe, and when your children's children think themselves alone in the field, the store, the shop, upon the highway, or in the silence of the pathless woods, they will not be alone... At night when the streets of your cities and villages are silent and you think them deserted, they will throng with the returning hosts that once filled them and still love this beautiful land. The White Man will never be alone'.

Left: espresso coffee fuels Seattle's vigorous urban life. The calorie-conscious can order a 'skinny' latte – an espresso with steamed, non-fat milk
Above: The Seattle Times masthead

Seattle Life

One of the imposing totem poles that decorate Pioneer Square

BILL GATES

Seattle's best-known man is also currently the world's richest. Born in 1956, Bill Gates grew up in Seattle and attended the city's most prestigious private school. During high school, Gates met fellow student Paul Allen. They went on to found Microsoft, the world's most successful software company, which still has its world headquarters in suburban Seattle.

announced plans to move its corporate headquarters out of Seattle – a notion that would have been unthinkable a decade earlier. Together these unsettling events dampened the city's cockiness, so that today, the city has finally come of age.

Seattle's population represents a diverse cultural mix. Ethnic minorities constitute 32 per cent of the overall population. Asian influence is felt in a Northwest aesthetic reminiscent of Japan – in city gardens, fountains and architecture – and in the sizeable number of Asian restaurants and markets. Despite its relative affluence, Seattle's population, sad to say, also includes a large number of homeless people.

As for the weather, most Seattleites take it in their stride. Few let the drizzle slow them down and real natives secretly scoff at those who carry umbrellas. This 'no worries' attitude extends to other things as well: while angst-ridden bands like Nirvana emerged in the early 1990's as a reaction to the city's 'laid-back' style, nevertheless, Seattle's attitude of tolerance enabled grunge music to flourish.

Today, grunge is history. While many residents still prize informality and irreverence, the expanding population and personal wealth have created greater fashion-conciousness and big-city sophistication. Cultural institutions are thriving. Outside of New York, Seattle has the greatest number of professional theatre companies in the United States. Seattle Symphony has moved into a grand new hall with outstanding acoustics; the Opera and Pacific Northwest Ballet will move into a splendid remodelled facility in 2003.

Not surprisingly, in a city so blessed by its natural surroundings, environmental consciousness is high. Seattle has won kudos for its recycling programme. It's tough on smokers, though, as all public buildings and many workplaces and restaurants ban smoking.

So pack your opera glasses and hiking boots, throw away that umbrella, and prepare to do Seattle like a native.

Seattle in Figures

Population
- Seattle: 563,374 (aged 18 and older 475,547; with college degrees 37.9 per cent).
- Metropolitan area including Everett, Tacoma and Bremerton: 2.6 million.
- Historic growth: 1878: 2,000; 1890: 42,000; 1910: 237,194; 1930: 365,583; 1950: 467,591; 1970: 530,831; 1990: 516,259.
- Of the 47,115 residents new to the city since 1990, more than half were Hispanic and Asian.

The City
- Latitude: 47°36'32"N.
- Longitude: 122°20'12"W.
- Depth of Elliott Bay: 150–900 feet.
- Number of hills: 12; highest point: West Seattle (512 feet).
- Total square miles: 91.6 (88.5 land; 3.1 water).
- Parks: more than 300, totalling 5,000 acres.
- Rainfall: 34–37 inches per year.
- Number of clear days: 56 per year.

Firsts
- Gas station (1907).
- Public golf course in the United States (1915).
- General strike in the United States (1919).
- Circumnavigational flight from Sandpoint Naval Station (1924).
- Woman mayor (Bertha Landes; 1924).
- Water skis (1928).
- Concrete 'floating' bridge (1939).
- Full-scale monorail (1962).
- Covered shopping mall (1950).

The REI store

A Chronology

1792	British Captain George Vancouver and his lieutenant, Peter Puget, explore the 'inland sea', which Vancouver names Puget Sound.
1851	David Denny, John Low and Lee Terry reach Alki Point and dub their colony 'New York–Alki'.
1852	Pioneers move the settlement across Elliott Bay to what is now Pioneer Square.
1853	Henry Yesler begins operating a steam sawmill, establishing the timber industry. President Fillmore signs an act creating the Washington Territory. (Achieves statehood 1889.)
1855	The Point Elliott Treaty, signed by Governor Isaac Stevens, Chief Sealth and others, banishes Native Americans to reservations.
1856	'The Indian War': American battle sloop *Decatur* fires into downtown to root out native peoples, who burn the settlement.
1861	The University of Washington is established.
1864	Asa Mercer returns from New England with 11 young women (the Mercer Girls) as wives for lonely Seattle bachelors.
1869	The city is incorporated and passes its first public ordinance – a law against drunkenness.
1886	Anti-Chinese riots erupt.
1889	The Great Seattle Fire caused damage exceeding $10 million.
1893	James Hill's Great Northern Railroad reaches its western terminus, Seattle.
1897	The ship *Portland* steams into Seattle carrying 'a ton of gold' and triggers the Klondike Gold Rush. Seattle becomes the primary outfitting centre for prospectors.
1903	The Seattle Symphony Orchestra is formed.

1907	Pike Place Public Market opens.
1909	Seattle hosts Alaska-Yukon-Pacific Exposition.
1909–1917	Lake Washington Ship Canal is built.
1914	The 42-storey Smith Tower is completed.
1919	The Seattle General Strike: 60,000 workers walk off the job.
1926	Bertha Landes is elected mayor, the first woman mayor of a major American city.
1940	The Lake Washington Floating Bridge links Seattle with Eastside communities.
1941	US entry into World War II. Workers flood into Seattle to work in the shipyards and elsewhere.
1949	An earthquake measuring 7.2 on the Richter scale rocks the area.
1962	Seattle hosts the Century 21 World's Fair.
1963	A second floating bridge, the 1.4-mile Evergreen Point Bridge, is completed.
1970	Boeing lays off 655,000 workers over a two-year period, precipitating a recession.
1971	Starbucks opens in Pike Place Market, launching the nation's speciality coffee craze.
1975	William Gates and Paul Allen start Microsoft.
1980	Mount St Helens erupts, showering ash over Seattle, 100 miles away.
1999	World Trade Organization (WTO) meets in Seattle. Protestors take to the streets.
2000	US Justice Department anti-trust ruling orders breakup of Microsoft. Microsoft appeals.
2001	Boeing announces plans to move corporate HQ.

11

People & Events from History

A bust of Chief Sealth in Pioneer Square

BEYOND SIGN LANGUAGE

Early explorers, traders and Native Americans communicated in Chinook, a language that developed as a trade medium. Seattle pioneers mastered Chinook, and it served as the common language with local tribes. Here are a few everyday terms:

tillicum = friend
illahee = land
klootchman = woman
potlatch = gift
muck-a-muck = food
chickamin = money
chee chacko = newcomer
mashie! = thank you

CHIEF SEALTH

Sealth was born in 1786 on Blake Island. In 1792, the young boy watched 'the great canoe with giant white wings' – Captain Vancouver's three-masted brig – sail into Puget Sound. In his 20s, he became leader of the Suquamish, Duwamish and allied bands, and became a friend to white settlers – so much so that pioneer Arthur Denny suggested changing the settlement's name from 'Alki' to 'Sealth'. Since the name was difficult for whites to pronounce properly, it became corrupted to 'Seattle'.

THE BIRTH OF TRADE

In December 1852, the brig *Leonesa* sailed into Seattle hoping to find timber for rebuilding parts of San Francisco destroyed by fire. The pioneers had none, but in the next few days, they worked feverishly, cutting trees and hauling them to the waterfront. At this moment, a realisation was born: the great forests of the Northwest, hitherto viewed as obstacles to growth, were now seen as a valuable and plentiful resource. Seattle's tie to both timber and trade was assured. The following year, Henry Yesler began operation of the first steam sawmill, firmly establishing the importance of lumber in the region's economy.

THE POINT ELLIOTT TREATY

Preceeding the Indian War of 1856, Territorial Governor Isaac Stevens drafted a settlement and persuaded Chief Sealth and other Native American leaders to sign. The Point Elliott Treaty promised the tribes payments, services and reservation lands. Fearing that his people would be absorbed by the growing numbers of settlers, Sealth reluctantly signed. In a speech, Chief Sealth imagined his people 'ebbing away like a rapidly receding tide that will never return'. He implored the whites to 'be just and deal kindly with my people, for the dead are not powerless'.

SEATTLE
how to organise your time

ITINERARIES *14–15*
Downtown
Seattle Center to Fremont
Lake Union to the University
Waterfront to Bainbridge Island

WALKS *16–17*
City Centre to Pike Place Market
Waterfront to Pioneer Square

EVENING STROLLS *18*
Green Lake
Myrtle Edwards/Elliott Bay Park

**ORGANISED
SIGHTSEEING** *19*

EXCURSIONS *20–21*
Mt Rainier
Victoria, British Columbia

Hurricane Ridge/
  Olympic National Park
Whidbey Island/La Conner

WHAT'S ON *22*

Itineraries

These itineraries can be undertaken on foot or by public transport. In good weather take a day trip out of the city (Excursions ➤ 20).

ITINERARY ONE	DOWNTOWN
Morning	Starting at the northwest corner of Pike Place Market (➤ 33), meander through the market, stopping at the stalls and shops. Work your way south to 1st and Union, then cross the street and continue one block south to the Seattle Art Museum (➤ 36).
Lunch	Eat at the market, the museum café or across 1st by the Harbor Steps (➤ 54).
Afternoon	Catch bus 174 southbound on 2nd to the world-class Museum of Flight (➤ 43). Return the same way, but get off close to Pioneer Square (➤ 39), at 4th and Jackson.
Evening	Enjoy an Italian dinner in Pioneer Square or go to nearby Shanghai Garden in the International District (➤ 41). For entertainment, consider a ballgame (➤ 83), music clubs (➤ 80–81) or stand-up comedy (➤ 81) in the area.
ITINERARY TWO	SEATTLE CENTER TO FREMONT
Morning	Ride the monorail to Seattle Center (➤ 35). In clear weather, go up the Space Needle for a view (➤ 30), then visit the Pacific Science Center (➤ 29) where science is brought to life with the use of interactive displays.
Lunch	For something simple and fast, grab a bite at the Center House foodcourt. If the weather's good, have a picnic by the fountain. For a more formal lunch, try neighbourhood restaurants or EMP's Turntable Restaurant.
Afternoon	Stroll the Center House grounds. For an interactive musical experience, check out the Experience Music Project (➤ 31) before catching bus 82 (1st and Denny) to the offbeat neighbourhood of Fremont (➤ 55).

ITINERARY THREE | **LAKE UNION TO THE UNIVERSITY**

Morning

At the Westlake Center, catch bus 70, 71, 72 or
73 to Lake Union (➤ 37). Exit on the
south/southeast side between Yale Landing
and Chandler's Cove. Rent a small boat and go
out on the water or else take a guided tour.

Lunch

Try one of the many restaurants on the eastern
shore.

Afternoon

Catch bus 70, 71, 72 or 73 to the University of
Washington (➤ 44), and visit the Burke
Museum (➤ 46). Then relax in the café or in
the fossil courtyard before walking to Red
Square and going to the Henry Art Gallery
(➤ 45). Leave the campus via Rainier Vista,
noting the great view, and catch the 25 bus
along Montlake Boulevard. If you have the
time and the energy, stop along the way at the
REI outdoor store (➤ 40). Afterwards, with
your bus transfer slip, re-board the 25 bus for
the city centre.

ITINERARY FOUR | **WATERFRONT TO BAINBRIDGE ISLAND**

Morning

From Pike Place Market (➤ 33), walk down
the Hillclimb to the Seattle Aquarium (➤ 32),
then continue south along the water to catch
the ferry to Bainbridge Island (➤ 34).
Walk the half-mile into town and stick your
head into the shops along Winslow Way.

Lunch

Eat in town at Café Nola (➤ 68) or buy a treat
from Bainbridge Bakery.

Afternoon

Visit Bainbridge Island Winery (➤ 59) to
sample local wines. If you have a car, drive to
Bloedel Reserve for an afternoon walk (reservations are required) or cross Agate Pass to
Suquamish Museum.

Evening

Drop in at the Harbour Public House (➤ 82),
where the locals go for fish and chips, then ride
the ferry back as the sun sets.

Walks

THE SIGHTS

- Freeway Park (➤ 50)
- Rainier Square
- Blueprints: 100 Years of Seattle Architecture – free exhibit by the Museum of History and Industry (➤ 52)
- Fifth Avenue Theater (➤ 54)
- City Center (➤ 35)
- Westlake Center
- Westlake Park
- Pike Place Market (➤ 33)

CITY CENTER TO PIKE PLACE MARKET

Begin at the Seattle/King County Visitor Center on the galleria level of the Washington State Convention and Trade Center. Pick up a calendar of events and a discount coupon book; then walk to the central lobby, where you'll pass under an imposing carved Native doorway ('Kwakiutl' tribe) to board the escalator to level 4. Take a moment to peruse the art display to both sides of the escalator. Exit through Freeway Park to the park's southwest corner. Descend the concrete stairs through the Canyon waterfall, designed to mask traffic noise from the freeway underneath. Leave the park at 6th and University, cross University, and climb the stairs to Union Square for a view of the city from the spacious plaza. Now double back to University, heading west to Rainier Square. Have a look at the Seattle architecture exhibit – level 3 – and exit on 5th across from the Fifth Avenue Theater (➤ 54) and Eddie Bauer (➤ 70). Head north across Union, past the City Center, and cross Pike and Pine to the Westlake Center.

Coffee break Look left for the glass-walled Seattle's Best Coffee, opposite Westlake Park, a good place to stop for a coffee.

Freeway Park's waterfall

INFORMATION

Distance 1–1½ miles
Start point The Washington Convention Center, 8th and Pike
✚ E6
🚌 7, 10, 43 on Pike
End point Harbor Steps, University Street between 1st Avenue & Western
✚ F6
🚋 Waterfront streetcar

The market Head down Pine to 1st. Walk north one block to Stewart, go left for half a block to Post Alley, and right down the narrow way to Virginia. Stroll past Pike Place Fish, where the clerks and countermen hurl salmon through the air. Continue south until you are facing Tenzing Momo Herbal Apothecary; then head down the stairs on your left, winding along an interior corridor past Pike Place Brewery until you come out at 1st and Union across from Seattle Art Museum. One block south, at 1st Avenue and University, you'll reach Harbor Steps (➤ 54).

WATERFRONT TO PIONEER SQUARE

Stroll down the Harbor Steps and amble south along the Waterfront to Yesler. Turn left and walk to the corner of 1st and Yesler, site of Pioneer Square's pergola (renovated in 2001). Smith Tower is one block east. Cross to the east side of 1st and walk south, taking time to drift into shops along the way. Cross Washington, pass Grand Central Arcade, and continue across Main to the Elliott Bay Bookstore and Café. Stop for a coffee or to browse the bookshelves, then proceed along 1st to Jackson and go left one block to cobblestoned Occidental, then left again onto its pedestrian mall. Step into the shops and galleries along the way, and if possible, catch a glass-blowing demonstration at Glasshouse Art Glass.

After the goldrush At Main, visit the Klondike Gold Rush National Historic Park, just left of Occidental. The museum commemorates Seattle's role as an outfitting centre for prospectors. As you exit, turn right and walk past Occidental Park, noting the totem poles, and continue to Waterfall Park, a serene oasis at 2nd Avenue. Walk right on 2nd one block to Jackson to see the lovely 'Rain Forest Gate'. Head back by catching a bus northbound on 2nd Avenue or walk southeast to Metro's International District bus station. Exit at University and drop in at the lobby of Benaroya Hall, home of the Seattle Symphony, to see the enormous chandeliers by NW artist Dale Chihuly.

Falcons on TV Now, take a walk to Washington Mutual's blue tower (► 54) at 3rd and Seneca, where a video camera poised on the rooftop records the activities of two peregrine falcons that return each year to nest. End your tour by walking up hill for one block to the elegant Four Seasons Olympic Hotel, where you can relax and enjoy a drink in the Terrace Room.

THE SIGHTS

- Waterfront (► 32)
- Pioneer Square (► 39)
- Smith Tower (► 54)
- Glasshouse Art Glass (► 58)
- Klondike Gold Rush National Historic Park
- Occidental Park totems (► 53)
- Waterfall Park
- Safeco Field
- Washington Mutual Building (► 54)

INFORMATION

Distance 1–1½ miles
Start point Harbor Steps, 1st Avenue and University Street
🚇 F6
🚋 Waterfront Streetcar
End point Four Seasons Olympic Hotel, 4th and University
🚇 F6
🚌 Free bus zone

Pioneer Square street scene

Evening Strolls

Join the locals for an evening stroll around Green Lake Park

GREEN LAKE

An evening stroll around Green Lake is a great way to watch Seattleites doing what they like most – relaxing outdoors. On fine days, you'll see a whole cross-section of energetic types, including bikers, joggers, speed-walkers, dog-walkers, skaters and Frisbee-players. The paved 2.8-mile loop that encircles the lake has two lanes – one for pedestrians, the other for people on wheels – and a variety of lovely old trees provide shade along the way.

Everyone from toddlers to seniors training for one last marathon converge on the Green Lake trail, and ducks and Canada geese compete with humans for sovereignty of the coveted grassy areas. Along the trail, you'll pass the old Bathhouse Theater, two swimming beaches, a golf course, fishing piers, boat rentals, tennis courts and a community centre and pool.

ELLIOTT BAY TRAIL

This 2½ mile walking and biking trail begins on the north end of the pier 70 car park at Myrtle Edwards Park and winds along the water through Elliott Bay Park. Soon, the divided path swings around three huge granite slabs, which together make up Michael Heizer's controversial sculpture *Adjacent, Against, Upon.* Continuing north, you'll pass the enormous grain terminal and loading dock where wheat and other grain brought in by rail from eastern Washington and the Midwest is loaded onto ships bound for foreign ports. The trail continues through Elliott Bay Park and terminates just past a public fishing dock.

INFORMATION

Green Lake
Distance About 3 miles
Start and end point car park, Green Lake Community Center (East Green Lake Drive)
➕ Off map K2, L2
🚍 16, 26

Myrtle Edwards/Elliott Bay Park
Distance 2½ miles
Start and end point Pier 70 at Broad Street and Alaskan Way, north end of the car park
➕ D2
🚍 1 or 2 (to 1st and W Bay), 13, 15, 18; waterfront trolley

Organised Sightseeing

ON THE WATER

Argosy Tours (☎ 206/623–4252, www.argosycruises.com).
One-hour harbour cruises; 2½-hour tours through
the lakes and Hiram M Chittenden Locks (pier
57) and the 'Sleepless in Seattle' Lake Union/
Lake Washington loop. Over the holidays, Argosy
operates 'Christmas Ship' cruises. Pier 55–56 for
harbour cruises; lake cruises from 1200 Westlake.
Discover Houseboating (☎ 206/322–9157). Person-
alised tours on Lake Union (Walking tours also).
Spirit of Puget Sound (☎ 206/674–3500). Lunch,
dinner and moonlight cruises on Elliott Bay. Buffet,
shows and dance bands. Daily from pier 70.

ON LAND

Gray Line Tours (☎ 206/626–5208 or 800/426–7505).
City bus tours; 'Grapes and Hops' to winery and
brewery; Boeing tours; day and overnight trips to
Mt Rainier, Vancouver, Victoria, BC, the Olympic
Peninsula and the San Juan Islands. Depart from
desk at Washington State Convention Center.
Seattle Tours (☎ 206/768–1234). Tours of down-
town area in mini-coaches (9:30AM and 2PM).
Day trips to Mt Rainier National Park run
May–October and include walks and hikes in
the Northwest wilderness. Also available to
Mt St Helens and the Olympic Peninsula.
Viewpoints Architectural Walking Tours (☎ Tour
Hotline: 206/667–9186). Walking tours to a variety of
downtown and residential sites, May–Nov.

WATER AND LAND

Ride the Ducks (☎ 206/441–3825). Seattle's most
novel downtown tour in a World War II amphibi-
ous landing craft. The tour takes in Pioneer
Square, the market and the waterfront by land
before plunging into Lake Union.

FROM THE AIR

Seattle Seaplanes (☎ 206/329–9638 or 1–800/637–5553).
Flights over Seattle and environs. Daily depar-
tures from east shore of Lake Union.
Kenmore Air Seaplanes (☎ 425/486–1257;
1–800/543–9595; www.kenmoreair.com). Daily flights
from the South Lake Union terminal to Victoria,
BC or the San Juan Islands.

TILLICUM VILLAGE/ BLAKE ISLAND

This four-hour excursion to
Blake Island, which includes a
narrated harbour tour, salmon
dinner and stunning theatrical
presentation of Native
American legend, touches on
nearly every highlight of the
Northwest: you'll see views
and lush vegetation, and get a
chance to ply the waters, hike
forest trails, experience Native
American culture and sample
quality entertainment. Year-
round from pier 56.
☎ 206/443–1244.

Excursions

INFORMATION

Mt Rainier
Distance 90 miles southeast of Seattle
Journey time 3 hours by road
Route I-5 south to Tacoma; east on 512; south on route 7 and east on route 706 to the park entrance
Bus tours Gray Line (☎ 206/624–5813) or Scenic Bound Tours (☎ 206/433–6907)
Mt Rainier National Park (☎ 360/569–2211)
Paradise Visitor Center (☎ 360/589–2275)

Victoria, British Columbia
Journey time 2–3 hours, one-way
Victoria Clipper (☎ 206/448–5000)

The Empress Hotel dominates Victoria's pretty harbourfront

The excursions in this section are most easily done by car. The Hurricane Ridge and Whidbey Island trips require ferry rides; keep in mind that delays can be considerable at the terminals, especially in summer and on weekends.

MT RAINIER

Known simply as 'the mountain', Mt Rainier is the jewel in the crown of Washington's peaks. It rises 14,410 feet above sea level, and the upper 6,000 to 7,000 feet are covered in snow and ice year-round. On clear Seattle days, its white dome hovers over the city with an awesome presence so immediate, it's hard to believe it's 70 miles away. Small wonder that native peoples ascribed supernatural power to this active volcano, one of a string running south from the Canadian border to California. Since there's no public transport to Mt Rainier, plan to drive and explore on your own, or take one of the bus tours. For a birds-eye-view of Mt Ranier, drive to Crystal Mountain and take the chairlift to its summit. From here there is a staggering view of Mt Ranier. For information on hiking, stop at Longmire, then drive 11 miles to the Paradise Visitor Center, the take-off point for various hikes. (The centre is open daily but hours vary seasonally.)

VICTORIA, BRITISH COLUMBIA

Cruise northern Puget Sound and the Strait of Juan de Fuca aboard the passenger only *Victoria Clipper*, a high-speed catamaran, and sail directly into Victoria's beautiful Inner Harbor. Tourists pour into this provincial capital for a taste of merry England, and Victoria obliges with formal gardens, double-decker buses and shops selling tweeds and Irish linen. If that's not your cup of tea, it's still a lovely trip, especially with a window seat on the *Clipper's* upper deck. See the excellent Northwest Coast artefacts at the Royal British Columbia Museum and, if you choose, meander through the ever-popular Butchart Gardens or indulge yourself with tea in the imperial splendour of the Empress Hotel. Multiple daily roundtrips provide visitors some flexibility in determining how long to stay in Victoria.

HURRICANE RIDGE/OLYMPIC NATIONAL PARK

Take the ferry to Bainbridge Island (➤ 34). From there, take 305 west to 3 north, then pick up 104. Follow 20 to Port Townsend, pausing for coffee or lunch in this Victorian town before doubling back to 101 west and Port Angeles. Turn south on Hurricane Ridge Road and drive the 17 winding miles to the Olympic National Park Visitor Center. Walk the 1½-mile trail to Hurricane Hill, watching for marmot and deer. To see the Elwha River rainforest, return to Port Angeles, continuing west on 101 the short distance to Olympic Hot Springs Road. Feast your eyes on the lush vegetation and watch for elk. From here, retrace the route to Seattle, and if time and energy permit, walk Dungeness Spit. If you're hungry, break up your return trip by stopping at Fat Smittys for a burger (located on Discovery Day) or feast on local Dungeness crab at Three Crabs on Route 101, and call it a day.

WHIDBEY ISLAND/LA CONNER

Drive past Boeing's 747 plant (➤ 48) to Mukilteo. Take the Whidbey ferry, then drive into Langley for exploration, coffee and goodies. Take 20 north, turning off at Fort Casey to climb the battlements and walk the bluff. Continue to the charming town of Coupeville, dating back to 1852, for something to eat, and proceed north to dramatic Deception Pass. For a picnic or walk on the beach, follow the signs to state beaches, mostly littered with washed-up logs. Continue on 20, swinging east to the Farmhouse Inn, and turn right onto Best Road. Drive through farmland to the 19th-century town of La Conner. Explore on your own, then stop for refreshments before heading southeast to Conway and I-5 southbound.

INFORMATION

Hurricane Ridge/Olympic National Park
Distance 190 mile round trip
Journey time: 2½ hours by road to Port Townsend (a long day trip)
Route Ferry to Bainbridge Island, west through Kitsap to the Olympic Peninsula
Olympic National Park Visitor Center
    ☎ 360/452–0330

INFORMATION

Whidbey Island/La Conner Loop
Distance 160 mile loop
Journey time A long day trip
Route I-5 north to Mukilteo ferry; on Whidbey, route 525 to 20 north
🔁 Skagit Valley tulip fields– April is peak season–for information and maps call 800/488–5477

21

What's On

January	*Chinese and Vietnamese New Year's Celebration. Martin Luther King Celebration.*
February	*Fat Tuesday.* A week-long Mardi Gras celebration in Pioneer Square.
March	*Imagination Celebration/Art Festival for Kids. Seattle Fringe Festival.*
April	*Cherry Blossom and Japanese Cultural Festival.*
May	*Opening Day of Yachting Season* (first Saturday): races on Lakes Union and Washington. *International Children's Theater Festival:* Performances by groups from around the world. *University Street Fair:* Crafts and entertainment. *Northwest Folklife Festival:* The largest folk festival in the country. *Pike Place Market Festival:* Food, music, crafts. *Seattle International Film Festival.*
June	*Fremont Solstice Parade and Celebration* (21 June): Elaborate costumes and floats to celebrate the longest day of the year. *Fremont Arts and Crafts Fair:* Crafts, food. *Out to Lunch Summer:* Downtown concerts. *Summer Nights on the Pier:* Concert series.
July	*Fourth of July:* Fireworks over Lake Union and Elliott Bay. *Lake Union Wooden Boat Festival. Caribbean Festival–A Taste of Soul:* Food, music. *Chinatown International District Summer Festival:* Performances, food, crafts. *Bite of Seattle Food Fest. Pacific Northwest Arts and Crafts Fair. Seafair:* Everything from milk-carton derbies and hydrofoil heats to Indian pow-wows.
September	*Bumbershoot:* Festival of music, visual arts, crafts.
October	*Northwest Bookfest:* Literary festival.
December	*Christmas Ship:* Brightly lit vessels make the rounds of the beaches with vocal groups aboard who sing carols to people along the shore.

SEATTLE's
top 25 sights

The sights are shown on the maps on the inside front cover and inside back cover, numbered **1** – **25** from west to east across the city

1 Discovery Park *24*

2 Alki Beach *25*

3 The Hiram M Chittenden Locks *26*

4 Fishermens' Terminal *27*

5 Woodland Park Zoo *28*

6 Pacific Science Center *29*

7 Space Needle *30*

8 Experience Music Project *31*

9 The Waterfront & Aquarium *32*

10 Pike Place Market *33*

11 Ferry to Bainbridge Island *34*

12 Monorail to Seattle Center *35*

13 Seattle Art Museum *36*

14 Lake Union *37*

15 Downtown *38*

16 Pioneer Square *39*

17 REI (Recreational Equipment Inc) *40*

18 The International District *41*

19 Volunteer Park *42*

20 Museum of Flight *43*

21 University of Washington *44*

22 Henry Art Gallery *45*

23 Burke Museum of Natural History and Culture *46*

24 Washington Park Arboretum *47*

25 The Boeing Tour *48*

Discovery Park

INFORMATION

Discovery Park

- ✚ Off map L2; Locator map A3
- ✉ 3801 W Government Way
- ☎ 206/386–4236
- 🕐 Park daily dawn to dusk. Visitor Center daily 8:30–5 except national holidays
- 🚍 33
- ♿ Poor
- 🆓 Free
- ℹ Nature walks and classes; children's playground

Daybreak Star Art Center

- ☎ 206/285–4425
- 🕐 Mon–Fri 9–5; Sat 10–5; Sun noon–5
- ♿ Very good
- ℹ Salmon lunch/Artmart, Sat in Dec; Seafair Indian Pow-Wow Days, third weekend in July

Detail of one of the artworks inside
Daybreak Star

This park is the largest stand of wilderness in the city. Its meadows, forests, cliffs, marshes and shoreline provide habitat for many birds and animals.

Legacy of the military The 520 forested acres on Magnolia Bluff that is today's Discovery Park was a military base from the 1890s, but in 1970, the government turned it over to the city for use as a park. During the transfer, an alliance of local tribes decided to take the opportunity to regain ancestral land they felt was theirs, and eventually, 19 acres were set aside for a Native American cultural centre.

Discover the trails The park's great size means that there are miles of nature, and bike trails to be explored. Test your fitness along the ½ mile 'parcours' (health path) through the woods. To the west, 2 miles of beach extend north and south from the West Point lighthouse (head south for sand, north for rocks). To get to the beach, pick up the loop trail at the north or south car park. The park's Visitor Center provides free 90-minute walks led by a naturalist, every Saturday at 2PM.

Daybreak Star Art Center The structure uses enormous cedar timbers to reflect the points of a star. Native art adorns the walls inside. The Center's Sacred Circle Gallery of American Indian Art is one of only four showcases dedicated to contemporary Native American work in the country.

Alki Beach

Alki beach is Seattle's birthplace. Today, its sandy shore and waterfront trail are as close as Seattle gets to resembling Southern California.

Beginnings The Duwamish and Suquamish peoples were on hand to meet the schooner *Exact* when it sailed into Elliott Bay on 13 November 1851. The ship anchored off Alki Point and Arthur Denny and his party of 23 paddled their skiff ashore. The locals proved friendly and the Denny party decided to stay. They set about building four log cabins, wistfully naming their new home New York–Alki, 'Alki' being a word in the Chinook language for 'someday', an indication of Denny's ambitions. The following year, after surviving fierce winter storms, the settlers decided to move across Elliott Bay to the more sheltered, deepwater harbour that is today's Pioneer Square.

Beach life The beach itself is the main attraction today. There are great views, fine sand, a paved trail, and boat and bike rentals. There's food and drink, too – try Pegasus (for pizza) and the Alki Bakery (for cookies and other sweets). You can walk, bike or skate the 2½ miles from Alki Beach to Duwamish Head. If you wish, continue south along the water to lovely Lincoln Park where an outdoor saltwater pool and waterslide invite a refreshing dip (▶ 51).

INFORMATION

✚ Off map L2;
Locator map A4
✉ 3201 Alki Avenue SW (Alki Point Light Station)
☎ 206/217–6124
🕐 Lighthouse Sat–Sun noon–4 and some holidays. Coast Guard officer on duty May–Aug to answer questions
🚌 37 from 2nd Avenue (no night or weekend service); 56 southbound on 1st Avenue
♿ Wheelchair access along paved trail
↔ Lincoln Park (▶ 51)
ℹ Bike, inline skate and boat hire (▶ 56–57); driftwood fires permitted on beach

The Alki Point Light Station looks across Puget Sound

The Hiram M Chittenden Locks

Above: the turbulent waters of the Chittenden Locks

Legions of boat owners pass through these locks when taking their boats from freshwater into Puget Sound. Alongside, salmon struggle to climb a fish ladder on the miraculous return to their spawning grounds.

A dream comes true The 1917 opening of the Ballard Locks and Lake Washington Ship Canal was the fulfillment of a 60-year-old pioneer dream to build a channel that would link Lake Washington and Puget Sound. Primitive construction attempts were made in the 1880s, but it wasn't until Major Hiram M Chittenden, regional director of the Army Corps of Engineers, won Congressional approval in 1910, that work began in earnest. Over the next six years, workers excavated and moved thousands of tons of earth with giant steam shovels. The locks are operated from a control tower that regulates the spillway gates and flashes directions to boats. Displays in the nearby visitor centre explain the history and construction of the locks and ship canal. One-hour guided tours leave from the centre on weekends at 2PM.

Watch the fish A fish ladder, built into the locks, allows salmon and steelhead to move upstream from the sea to their spawning grounds. By sensing 'attraction water' at the fish ladder's entrance, the fish find the narrow channel and begin the long journey to the very freshwater spot where they began life. Here, they lay their eggs and die.

Botanical Gardens Nearby, you can also explore the 7-acre Carl S English Jr. Botanical Gardens, which are planted with more than 500 species from around the world.

Fishermen's Terminal

Fishermen's Terminal is a great place to soak up the comings and goings of a large fleet. Here, fishermen mend their nets and prepare to head north or return, tie up and unload their catch.

Early days Fish have been an important local resource since Seattle's early days, when the Shilshoh people from Salmon Bay first shared their bountiful harvest with other local tribes. With white settlement, fishing became an important local industry. In the early 1900s, a growing demand for salmon prompted the industry to lure new fishermen to the area – especially Scandinavian, Greek and Slavic immigrants – many of whose descendants still work in the fishing trade. In 1913, the Port of Seattle designated Fishermen's Terminal on Salmon Bay as home base for the North Pacific fishing fleet. Today Washington fishers harvest 50 per cent of all fish and other seafood caught in the United States.

Fishermen's Memorial Dominating the terminal's central plaza, a 30-foot-high column commemorates those Northwest fishermen who lost their lives at sea. Their names are inscribed at the memorial sculpture's base and serve to remind us that fishing was – and remains – extremely dangerous work and that the sea can be cruelly unforgiving.

DID YOU KNOW?

● More than 600 commercial fishing boats are based at the terminal, many bound for Alaska
   ● Gillnetters, purse seiners and trawlers use nets; ongliners and trollers use lines
   ● Trollers have a mid-ship pole, hung at a 45-degree angle, to which baited lines are secured

INFORMATION

✚ Off map L2;
   Locator map A3
✉ 3919 18th Avenue Wat
   Salmon Bay
☎ 206/728-3395
🕐 24 hours
🚌 15 or 18 from 1st Avenue
   (Exit south of Ballard Bridge) or 33 from 4th Avenue
♿ Very good
🎫 Free
↔ Discovery Park (▶ 24)
ℹ Chinooks Restaurant, a wild fish market, gallery, grocery and marine shops

The Fishermen's Memorial is topped by a bronze sculpture of a halibut fisherman

Woodland Park Zoo

Woodland Park Zoo has won international recognition for its progressive design. The park allows animals to move freely in settings that resemble their natural habitats. The zoo maintains a captive breeding programme.

Running free (almost) Most animals roam freely in their simulated 'bioclimatic zones'. Four exhibits – African Savanna, Tropical Rain Forest, Northern Trail (Alaska) and Elephant Forest – have won prestigious awards and introduced zoo visitors not only to the animals, but also to corresponding plant species and ecosystems. The newest permanent exhibits include the amazing replica of an African village, an exhibit of the rare Dragons of Komodo, the world's largest lizards, and the Trail of Vines, which showcases macaques, tapirs, pythons and orang-utans in a setting representing the forests of western India and northern Borneo.

Zoo newcomers In the autumn of 2000, Seattleites welcomed a new 235-pound elephant calf, born on-site to the zoo's 22-year-old Asian female. More than 15,000 people submitted names of Thai origin to the zoo-sponsored naming contest: the winner was 'Hansa', meaning 'supreme happiness' in Thai. Less than a month earlier, a healthy, western lowland baby gorilla named Naku ('queen of the forest') was born.

Gorilla mother and child at Woodland Park Zoo

Pacific Science Center

As you approach the Pacific Science Center, you enter another world. Soaring gothic arches and an inner courtyard of reflecting pools, platforms and footbridges indicate you are in for something special.

Sputnik's legacy In 1962, the American scientific community was still smarting from the Soviet Union's unexpected launch of the Sputnik spacecraft. Determined to restore confidence in American science and technology, US officials pulled out all the stops when they built the US Science Pavilion for the Seattle World's Fair. The building reopened after the fair ended as the Pacific Science Center.

Science made easy A visit to the Pacific Science Center can happily fill half a day. The interactive exhibits bring scientific principles to life and make learning fun. In an outdoor exhibit, Water Works, you can manoeuvre a water cannon to activate whirligigs or attempt to move a 2-ton ball suspended on water. Near by, children can ride a high-rail bike for a bird's-eye view of proceedings. The Body Works exhibition lets you measure your stress level, grip strength and mental concentration, or see what your face looks like with two left sides. In the Tech Zone's Virtual Basketball installation, you stand against a backdrop, put on a virtual reality glove, and by moving an arm, transport yourself to a computer screen where you can go one-on-one against an on-screen opponent. Or, challenge a robot to a game of tic-tac-toe. The Science Playground and Brain Game areas use giant levers, spinning rooms and baseball batting cages to teach the principles of physics. Small children like blowing giant bubbles and climbing the rocket in the Kids' Zone. Next door is the IMAX 3-D Theater.

DID YOU KNOW?

- Designed by: Minoru Yamasaki
- Built as the US Science Pavilion for the 1962 World's Fair
- The first museum in the United States to be founded as a science and technology centre

INFORMATION

- D2; Locator map D2
- 200 2nd Avenue N (Seattle Center)
- 206/443–2001; website: www.pacsci.org
- Mon–Fri 10–5; Sat–Sun 10–6
- Fountains Café
- 1, 2, 3, 4, 13, 16, 24, 33
- Monorail
- Very good
- Moderate; half-price with CityPass (seniors free on Wed)
- Space Needle (➤ 30), Experience Music Project (➤ 31), Monorail (➤ 35),
- Two IMAX 3-D theaters; Laser Theater presents family matinees and evening rock shows

Above: hands-on fun at the Water Works exhibit

Space Needle

- The Space Needle sways about 1 inch for every 10mph of wind
- The Needle experienced an earthquake of 6.8 on the Richter scale (in 2001), and is equipped to withstand jolts up to 9.2

INFORMATION

➕ D3; Locator map D2
✉ Seattle Center
☎ 206/443–2111 or 800/937–9582
🕐 Observation Deck
Sun–Thu 9AM–11PM; Fri–Sat 9AM–midnight
🍴 Sky City Restaurant
Lunch/brunch Mon–Fri 11–3, Sat–Sun 9–3. Dinner Sun–Thu 4:30–9, Fri–Sat 4:30–10
🚌 3, 4, 16
🚈 Monorail
♿ Wheelchair access
💰 Expensive; half-price with CityPass; free with dinner at restaurant
🔄 Pacific Science Center (➤ 29), Experience Music Project (➤ 31), Monorail (➤ 35)

The Space Needle's height and futuristic design have made it Seattle's most well-known landmark. The view from the observation deck is stunning on a clear day.

The city's symbol The 605-foot Space Needle was built in 1962 for Seattle's futuristic World's Fair. Rising 200 feet above Seattle's highest hill, the structure is visible over a wide area. The steel structure weighs 3,700 tons and is anchored into the foundation with 72 huge bolts, each 32 feet long by 4 inches in diameter. The structure is designed to withstand winds up to 150mph, although the glass lifts are closed when winds top 60mph. If you ride in the glass-walled lift to the top during a snowstorm, it appears to be snowing upwards.

Observation deck Each year, more than a million visitors ride one of the three glass lifts to the observation deck at the 520-foot level. Informative displays point out more than 60 sites around the area and recount Space Needle facts and trivia. High-resolution

telescopes allow you to zoom in on objects for a closer view. A reservation at the Sky City Restaurant on the 500 level gets you to the observation deck free. Rotating one complete turn every hour, the Sky City Restaurant gives you a 360-degree panorama during the course of a meal.

A view of Seattle from the Needle's observation deck

Experience Music Project (EMP)

Seattle has entered the 21st century with a dazzling rock 'n' roll museum and musical gathering place. This temple to American music is unrivalled in both scale and daring.

EMP is Paul Allen's gift to the city. Co-founder of Microsoft, Allen idolised Seattle-born Jimi Hendrix and imagined a space to exhibit his personal collection of Hendrix memorabilia. Over time, the vision expanded beyond Hendrix: the museum would explore all of American popular music through interactive and interpretive exhibits.

The design Allen hired celebrated architect Frank O Gehry to create a structure that would reflect the rebelliousness that characterises rock 'n' roll. To jumpstart his design, Gehry cut up and rearranged several brightly-coloured electric guitars. This gave birth to EMP's bold colours, sweeping curves and reflective metal surface.

Inside The 85 foot 'Sky Church' features music film and video by day and live bands at night. Trace the development of the electric guitar or view artefacts of Seattle 'Grunge', jam on real instruments in the Sound Lab or record your own voice. On the Artist's Journey, travel the world of rock 'n' roll through image, sound, lighting, special effects and motion technology.

DID YOU KNOW?

- Jazz musician Les Paul pioneered electric guitar technology in Seattle by using a solid body. The Gibson company adopted the design and use it to this day
- Jimi Hendrix was born in Seattle in 1942. In the late 1960s he revolutionised electric guitar playing a radical fusion of jazz, rock, soul and blues

INFORMATION

- ✚ D3; Locator map D2
- ✉ Seattle Center
- ☎ 206/367–5483; www.emplive.com
- 🕐 Winter: Sun–Thu 10–6; Fri–Sat 10AM–11PM. Summer: daily 9AM–11PM
- 🚌 3, 4, 16
- ↔ Pacific Science Center (➤ 29), Space Needle (➤ 31), Monorail (➤ 35),
- ♿ Good
- 💲 Expensive

Jimi Hendrix, Seattle native and guitar hero

The Waterfront & Aquarium

HIGHLIGHTS

The aquarium
- Children's touch tank
- Underwater dome room
- Coral reef exhibit

The waterfront
- Bell Street complex restaurants and marina
- Waterfront trolley
- Odyssey Maritime Discovery Center
- Omnidome

INFORMATION

The aquarium
- ✚ F5; Locator map E3
- ✉ Pier 59: 1483 Alaskan Way at Pike Street
- ☎ 206/386–4300; recorded message: 206/386–4320
- 🕐 Jun–Aug: daily 10–7; Sep–May daily 10–5
- 🍴 Steamers Seafood Cafe on site
- 🚊 Waterfront streetcar (Pike Street station)
- ♿ Very good
- 💰 Moderate; half-price with CityPass
- ℹ️ For programme information see website: www.seattleaquarium.org

The waterfront
- ✉ Alaskan Way between Broad (pier 70) and Main (pier 48)
- 🚊 33; waterfront streetcar

Above: The aquarium's underwater dome

Seattle's history and economic growth have been closely tied to the waterfront since 1853, when Henry Yesler built the first sawmill at the foot of the hill that bears his name.

Starting out When pioneers settled along Elliott Bay's eastern shores in 1852, the only flat land suitable for building was a narrow strip along the water, where 1st Avenue runs today. A century later, Seattle's landscape had changed dramatically, after a large expanse of Elliott Bay was reclaimed. Maritime industrial activity had moved south to pier 46 and below, and the downtown waterfront was ripe for new beginnings.

Seattle Aquarium This is *the* place to acquaint yourself with Northwest marine life. In the underwater dome room you can watch Puget Sound's 'underworld' pass before your eyes. The Aquarium's newest exhibit features 'leafy sea dragons' – foot-long seahorses with what look to be greenish or golden branches. Other highlights include the exceptional Pacific coral reef exhibit and, for children who enjoy touching critters, the hands-on Discovery Lab.

Watery hub Import stores, restaurants and excursion boats dot the waterfront. The Odyssey Maritime Discovery Center at pier 66 (Bell St Complex) features interactive exhibits that illuminate the workings of a large port. At pier 36, the Coastguard office and museum explain the work of the coastguard. If your taste runs to the bizarre, head for Ye Olde Curiosity Shop, an antiques shop, and meet Sylvester the mummy. A picturesque trolley picks up passengers and drops them off along the waterfront, then loops north to Pioneer Square and the International District.

Pike Place Market

To many residents, Pike Place Market is Seattle's heart and soul. Here, people of every background converge, from city professionals and farmers to hippie craftsmen and tourists.

Farmers' market Pike Place Market was founded in 1907 so that farmers could sell directly to the consumer and eliminate the middleman. It was an immediate success, and grew quickly until World War II precipitated a decline. Threatened by demolition in the 1960s, it's now protected as an Historic District.

Feast for the senses The three-block area stretching between Pike and Virginia has flowerstalls, fishsellers, produce displays, tea shops, bakeries, herbal apothecaries, magic stores and much more. Street musicians play Peruvian panpipes or sing the blues, and the fragrance of flowers and fresh bread fills the air. This is old Seattle frozen in time.

Exploring the market Pick up a map from the information booth (1st Avenue and Pike Street, near the big clock) and head out from the sculpture of Rachel the pig. Watch out for the flying fish (at Pike Place Fish), stop to admire the artfully arranged produce and flower displays, and make a sweep around the crafts area, where superb handmade items are sold.

HIGHLIGHTS

Market Arcade
● Shops: Read All About It (for newspapers), DiLaurenti's Grocery and Deli, Market Spice Teas, Tenzing Momo
● Restaurants: Athenian Inn, Sound View Café, Place Pigalle, Maximiliens

Sanitary Market Building/Post Alley
● Shops: Jack's Fish Spot, Milagros, Made in Washington

INFORMATION

➕ F5; Locator map E3
✉ 1st Avenue between Stewart and Union
☎ 206/682–7453
🕐 Mon–Sat 9–6; Sun 11–5. Closed some national holidays
🚍 Rt. 10 on Pine and 1st–4th Avenue (free ride zone); waterfront streetcar
♿ Poor
ℹ Market Theater Fri–Sun nights: www.unexpectedproductions.org
🔗 Seattle Aquarium (► 32), Seattle Art Museum (► 36), Pioneer Square (► 39)

Pike Place Fish Co is admired for its range of seafood

Ferry to Bainbridge Island

DID YOU KNOW?

- The island is 12 miles long and 4 miles wide
- Main towns: Winslow and Suquamish
- The Washington State ferry system is the world's largest

INFORMATION

Bainbridge Ferry
✚ E3, G5; Locator map E3
✉ Colman Dock, pier 52; Alaskan Way and Marion
☎ 206/464–6400, 1–800–84–33779 (for automated information); www.wsdot.wa.gov/ferries
🕐 From Seattle, 6AM–2AM; from Bainbridge, last ferry at 1:15AM
🚌 16, 66 to ferry; waterfront streetcar
♿ Some ferries
🍴 Moderate

Bainbridge Island Winery
✉ 682 Highway 305
☎ 206/842–9463
🕐 Tasting Wed–Sun noon–5. Tours year-round: Sun 2PM

Bloedel Reserve
✉ 7521 NE Dolphin Drive
☎ 206/842–7631
🕐 Wed–Sun 2–6
🍴 Free

There's nothing more delightful than catching a Washington State ferry to Bainbridge Island. Standing at the stern as the boat pulls away, you can see the entire Seattle skyline unfold.

The ferry It takes just 35 minutes to get to Bainbridge Island from the downtown waterfront. En route, you'll see an amazing panorama: the Seattle cityscape and Mt Rainier to the east, and Bainbridge Island and the snow-capped Olympic Range to the west.

Touring on foot Once you disembark at the Bainbridge ferry dock, walk the short distance to the town of Winslow, visit the charming boutiques, browse at Eagle Harbor Books, stop for lunch at Café Nola (► 69), or order treats from the Bainbridge Bakery. If it's Saturday, catch the market on the Winslow green, or, Wednesday to Sunday, visit Bainbridge's Island Winery for tasting. If you're synchronising your return with the sunset, you could linger at the Harbour Public House (► 82).

Touring by car or bike If you have wheels, visit Bloedel Reserve and walk the exquisite trails (call

in advance for reservations). Continuing across Agate Pass Bridge to the Kitsap Peninsula, you enter Port Madison Indian Reservation and the town of Suquamish, where Chief Sealth is buried. A museum shows the tribe's history.

The city drops away as the ferry heads to Bainbridge

Monorail to Seattle Center

Riding the Monorail to Seattle Center is like being in an old sci-fi movie. You buzz the city like a giant insect and sweep past Experience Music Project before alighting at the Center House.

World's Fair leftovers The Seattle Center district, like the monorail, is the legacy of the 1962 World's Fair. Once a Native American ceremonial ground, and later host to travelling circuses, the 74-acre site didn't assume its present form until the fair. The monorail has now run continuously longer than any other monorail in the world.

Museum city Every day, this elevated train carries up to 7,000 passengers between Westlake Center, Seattle's retail core and Seattle Center, its entertainment hub. There, you can go on amusement park rides, take a trip in the Space Needle's glass lift (► 30) or visit museums and galleries, including the Children's Museum (► 60), Experience Music Project (► 31), several craft galleries and the Pacific Science Center (► 29). Seattle Center is also home to opera, ballet, excellent theatre companies (► 78) and several professional sports teams. Also, Seattle's major festivals take place on the centre grounds. Stop in the Center House for something to eat or try one of the restaurants close by.

Easy walking Stroll through the delightful Sculpture Garden and the adjacent Peace Garden southwest of the Needle, or enjoy a picnic on the grass by the International Fountain.

INFORMATION

Monorail to Seattle Center

➕ E6; Locator map E3

✉ Downtown station 3rd floor, Westlake Center (5th Avenue at Pine Street); Seattle Center Station adjacent to EMP

☎ Seattle Center: 206/684–7200 or 206/684–8582; www.seattlecenter.com

🕐 Monorail daily every 10 minutes. Seattle Center grounds Mon–Fri 7:30–11PM; Sat–Sun 9–11PM

🍴 Seattle Center House. Closed Thanksgiving, Christmas and New Year.

🚍 3, 4, 16

♿ Free to Center grounds

The monorail station at Westlake Center

13

Seattle Art Museum

Some people love it; some can do without it. No one, however, fails to notice the imposing Seattle Art Museum or the 48-foot black metal sculpture that dominates its entrance.

Into another world The pink granite arcaded structure of the Seattle Art Museum (SAM), which opened in 1991, steps up the hill between 1st and 2nd Avenues. To reach the galleries, you ascend a grand staircase, walking the gauntlet between monumental paired rams, guardian figures and sacred camels from the Ming dynasty.

Dazzling collections SAM's permanent collections range from the indigenous art of Africa, Oceania and the Americas to modern US paintings and sculpture. Other galleries feature European painting and sculpture from the Medieval period through the 19th century. The Katherine White collection of African sculpture, masks, textiles and decorative arts is beautifully displayed, while a Northwest Coast collection features both small items, such as baskets and dream catchers, as well as much larger pieces, including four full-scale carved Kwakiutl house-posts. In other galleries, the museum presents travelling exhibitions and launches major shows of its own. Changing exhibitions feature ancient Chinese art from Sichuan, Annie Liebovitz photographs, African-American art and 20th-century art of Mexico.

Hammering Man Of the 48-foot sculpture out front sculptor Jonathan Borofsky has said: 'I want this work to appeal to all people of Seattle – not just artists, but families young and old. At its heart, society reveres the worker. *The Hammering Man* is the worker in all of us'.

HIGHLIGHTS

- Jonathan Borofsky's sculpture *Hammering Man*
- Indigenous art of Africa, Oceania and the Americas
- The Katherine White collection of African sculpture
- Northwest Coast collection

INFORMATION

- ✚ F5; Locator map E3
- ✉ 100 University Street
- ☎ 206/654–3100
- 🕐 Tue–Sun 10–5 (Thu 10–9). Closed Mon except holiday Mondays. Closed Thanksgiving, Christmas and New Year
- 🍴 Museum Café
- ☎ Through tunnel or along 1st, 2nd or 3rd (free-ride zone)
- ♿ Very good
- 💰 Moderate; half-price with CityPass. Admission ticket good for both downtown museum and Asian Art Museum in Volunteer Park. Free on first Thu of month; free for those over 62, first Fridays
- ↔ Waterfront (➤ 32), Pike Place Market (➤ 33), City Center (➤ 38), Pioneer Square (➤ 39), Harbor Steps (➤ 54)
- ❓ 'Thursday After Hours' features poetry and music

Lake Union

In a neighbourhood shared by tugboats and research ships, ducks and racoons, Lake Union's houseboaters swap dry land and backyards for a vibrant lifestyle on this bustling lake.

Floating world The houseboat life started over a century ago on Lake Union. A sawmill that opened on the lake in 1881 attracted a community of loggers and their hangers-on. Many of these woodsmen built themselves makeshift shelters by tying felled logs together and erecting tarpaper shacks on top. Before long, thousands of shacks floated on the waterways. These 'floating homes', Seattle's earliest houseboats, were a far cry from the gentrified versions made familiar by the film *Sleepless in Seattle*.

Boats and shops Today Lake Union is a lively mix of marine activity, houseboat living and expensive dining and shopping. Start your visit with a stroll, passing the 468-ton schooner *Wawona*, and the Center for Wooden Boats on the south end to get into the saltwater spirit. Then, for a true Lake Union experience, go out on the lake. You can hire sailboats, skiffs or kayaks, and explore on your own (▶ 57) or sign on with a tour (▶ 19). Back ashore, be sure to have a meal at one of the numerous good restaurants on Chandler's Cove.

DID YOU KNOW?

- Seattle has more houseboats than anywhere east of Asia, and most are on Lake Union
- Lake Union took its name from a pioneer's speech in which he dreamed that one day, a lake would form 'the union' between Puget Sound and Lake Washington
- Visitors who want to experience lakefront living can stay in a 'bunk and breakfast' anchored in the lake
- Gasworks Park on the north side offers great views of downtown and is the city's premier kite-flying spot

INFORMATION

- Locator map E1
- 70, 71, 72, 73 on Fairview/Eastlake
- Argosy Lake tours and 'Discover Houseboating' tours (▶ 19), Seattle Seaplanes and Kenmore Air (▶ 19), Kayak, rowing boat and sailboat hire (▶ 57)

A 'street' of houseboat homes on Lake Union

37

Downtown

These days, downtown is jumping. Old buildings have resurfaced as theatres, while new shops, restaurants and hotels continue to spring up.

Vertical Seattle The Seattle skyline began to change in the 1960's and by the mid 1980's more than two dozen new skyscrapers had dramatically altered the cityscape. Seattle's tallest building, the 76-storey Columbia Seafirst Center, is located at 4th Avenue and Cherry, between Seattle's commercial core and Pioneer Square.

Getting your bearings The phrase 'Downtown Seattle' is a rather ambiguous term that usually refers to a large area encompassing the Denny Regrade (Belltown), Pike Place Market, Pioneer Square and the International District. Seattle's retail core, however, is concentrated roughly in the centre between University and Stewart, and between 3rd and 7th Avenues. Most shops, restaurants, hotels and travel offices are clustered in and around Westlake Center, City Center, Rainier Square and Union Square.

Shopping Triangular Westlake Park, with its public art and curtain of water, is a popular gathering place, especially when steel bands are jamming. Across the square, Westlake Center lures shoppers with its food court and speciality shops. South of Westlake, chain stores like Abercrombie & Fitch, Niketown, FAO Schwartz and Banana Republic (➤ 70) have moved in, while a state-of-the-art video arcade, two multiplex cinemas and Planet Hollywood offer contemporary entertainment near by. Also check out City Center's exclusive shops, the Palomino Bistro (at 5th Avenue and Pike) and The Sharper Image, an emporium devoted to high-tech gadgets. At 5th and Union, you'll pass Eddie Bauer (➤ 70), America's first outdoor retailer.

DID YOU KNOW?

- In the early 1900's, more than half the wealth that was brought into Seattle during the Gold Rush days remained in the city
- John Nordstrom returned from the Yukon with $5,000 and pooled his resources with a partner's to open a shoe shop. Today, Nordstrom's downtown shop remains a cornerstone of the local retail economy

INFORMATION

Downtown Commercial Center

➕ Locator map E3

✉ Between 3rd and 7th Avenues, and Stewart and University Street

🚌 Through bus tunnel and on Pike, Pine, 3rd, 4th (free-ride zone)

🚃 Monorail, Westlake Center

♿ None

↔ Pike Place Market (➤ 33), Seattle Art Museum (➤ 36), Pioneer Square (➤ 39), Belltown (➤ 55), Freeway Park (➤ 50)

Pioneer Square

Constructed after the Great Seattle Fire, Pioneer Square's brick buildings retain an architectural integrity you won't find elsewhere in the city.

From the ashes In 1852, Seattle's pioneers moved across Elliott Bay and built the first permanent settlement in what is now Pioneer Square. The area burned to the ground in 1889, but was quickly rebuilt. When gold was discovered in the Yukon, prospectors converged on Pioneer Square to board ships to Alaska, and the area became the primary outfitting post for miners.

Moving through the square Pioneer Square's most notable landmarks include Smith Tower (► 54) and the lovely glass-and-iron pergola at 1st and Yesler (repaired in 2001). Interesting shops line 1st Avenue south of Yesler. Walk through the lovely Grand Central Arcade, which opens onto Occidental Park and cross Main Street, taking time to visit the Klondike Gold Rush National Historic Park. Take a short detour to enchanting Waterfall Park at 2nd and South Main; then backtrack to the bricked pedestrian walkway, and wander through Occidental Place, taking time to explore the cluster of art galleries that extend around the corner to 1st and South Jackson. Browse at Elliott Bay Book Company; then dine at one of the area's excellent restaurants, catch some live music or head for laughs at the Comedy Underground.

Nineteenth-century red-brick elegance at Pioneer Square

HIGHLIGHTS

- The pergola at 1st and Yesler
- Smith Tower
- Occidental Park and totem poles
- Klondike Gold Rush National Historic Park
- Waterfall Park
- The Elliott Bay Book Company bookstore

INFORMATION

Pioneer Square
- G6; Locator map E4
- Yesler to King and 2nd Avenue to Elliott Bay; Information booth in Occidental Mall in summer

Klondike Gold Rush National Historic Park
- 117 S Main
- 206/553–7220
- Daily 9–5
- 1st and 2nd Avenues (free-ride zone) and in bus tunnel (Pioneer Square Station). Waterfront trolley stop
- Wheelchair access
- Free
- Waterfront (► 32), Pike Place Market (► 33), Seattle Art Museum (► 36), International District (► 41), Harbor Steps (► 54)

REI (Recreational Equipment Inc.)

DID YOU KNOW?

- Lou Whittaker, general manager in the 1950s, was the first American to climb Everest
- REI is the largest retail co-operative in the United States, with over 1.4 million members
- The new REI building was constructed with materials that are either recycled or have minimal impact on the environment
- The Seattle store's 65-foot climbing pinnacle is the world's highest

INFORMATION

- D4; Locator map F2
- 222 Yale Avenue North
- 206/223–1944
- Mon–Fri 10–9; Sat 10–7, Sun 11–6
- World Wraps on site
- 70, 25, 66
- Good
- Pinnacle to climb (fee for non-members); educational programmes; equipment repair; equipment hire, travel service

The popularity of Recreational Equipment Inc, Seattle's premier retailer of outdoor wear and equipment, is legendary. The annual garage sale draws hordes of devotees who gather like pilgrims at a holy shrine.

It began with an ice axe REI had humble origins in the 1930s. It was founded by Seattle climber Lloyd Anderson, whose search for a high-quality, affordable ice axe ended in frustration – the one he wanted was not sold in the United States but could be ordered only from Europe. Anderson purchased one and soon his climbing buddies wanted their own. In 1938, 23 climbers banded together to form a member-owned co-operative in order to obtain mountaineering equipment unavailable in the United States.

Try it out REI's flagship store is *the* place to try before you buy. Under staff guidance, you can, for example, don a harness and scale the store's free-standing 65-foot high indoor pinnacle. There is a ' trail', where you can test the toughness of boots; another trail designed for mountain-bike test rides; and a 'rain room' where you can test the waterproof claims of the wide variety of outerwear. REI also carries a large selection of outdoor apparel and books.

Try out your skills and test the gear on the store's climbing pinnacle

The International District

Bordered by the sparkling Union Station office park and two sports stadiums, Seattle's International District is home to the city's Chinese, Japanese, Filipino, Southeast Asian, Korean and other Asian communities.

Multicultural mix The first Asian people to arrive in Seattle were Chinese men, who moved north from California to build the railways. Anti-Chinese riots broke out in the 1880s and many Chinese were deported, only to return after 1889 to help rebuild the charred settlement. The Japanese arrived next, many establishing small farms and selling their goods at Pike Place Market. The Filipinos, the third group to arrive, now constitute Seattle's largest Asian community.

The neighbourhood Smaller and more modest than San Francisco's Chinatown, the International District caters primarily to those who live and work in the neighbourhood. Start your exploration at the Wing Luke Museum to get a sense of Seattle's rich Asian and Pacific Island heritage. Permanent exhibits include 'One Song, Many Voices' which profiles the city's Asian cultures and Camp Harmony D-4-44, a replica of a Japanese internment camp. Before leaving the museum pick up a walking map of the neighbourhood. Make sure to include Hing Hay Park and Uwajimaya, the largest Asian emporium in the Northwest.

Eat city The district has many excellent Asian restaurants. Good bets include House of Hong for dim sum; Shanghai Garden for a Chinese lunch; or Yoshinobo for Japanese fare. For Vietnamese food, head up to 12th and Jackson ('Little Saigon') and try Saigon Bistro, or for Malaysian cuisine, check out Malay Satay at 12th and Main.

HIGHLIGHTS

- The many Asian restaurants
- Wing Luke Museum
- Hing Hay Park, with its ornate pavilion and dragon mural
- Uwajimaya, a large Asian emporium

INFORMATION

The International District
- E4; Locator map F4
- Between S Main and Lane Street and 5th and 8th Avenue S; 'Little Saigon' 12th S and Jackson.

Wing Luke Asian Museum
- 407 Seventh Avenue S
- 206/623–5124; www.wingluke.org
- Tue, Wed, Fri 11–4:30; Thu 11–7; Sat/Sun noon–4
- 1, 7 and 14 to Maynard and Jackson, 36 and bus tunnel (International District Station). Waterfront trolley to Jackson Street Station
- Wheelchair access for Museum only
- Inexpensive; free Thu
- Pioneer Square (➤ 39)
- Chinese New Year celebration in February

Volunteer Park

Volunteer Park offers more than a lush green space. There's a conservatory, a water tower to climb for views and Seattle's Asian Art Museum.

INFORMATION

Volunteer Park

- C4, C5; Locator map B3
- Between E Galer and E Prospect and 15th and 11th Avenues
- Park daily dawn to dusk. Conservatory summer: daily 10–7; rest of year daily 10–4
- Free
- 10, 7
- Poor

Seattle Asian Art Museum

- 1400 E Prospect
- 206/654–3100; www.seattleartmuseum.org
- Tue–Sun 10–5 (Thu 10–9). Closed Mon (except holiday Mondays), Thanksgiving, Christmas, New Year
- Fair
- Moderate; free first Thu and Sat of month, and first Fri for seniors. Free with SAAM admission

Above: a view from the park's water tower

Seattle Asian Art Museum (SAAM) Carl Gould's art-deco building once housed the entire Seattle Art Museum (SAM) collection (► 36). In 1991 SAM moved into a new downtown building, leaving the Volunteer Park museum to focus exclusively on Asian art. The extensive Chinese collection includes ancient burial ceramics, ritual bronzes, snuff bottles and a lovely Chinese Buddhist room, whose serene grey walls set off the gilded sculptures. Here you'll find the wonderful *Monk Caught at the Moment of Enlightenment*. SAAM also contains Korean, South and Southeast Asian collections, as well as a notable Japanese gallery which features a portion of an early 17th-century 'deer scroll', considered a Japanese national treasure. SAAM offers Sunday afternoon concerts and dance programmes, often in the central Garden Court. After touring the museum, you can sample your choice of teas in the Kado Tearoom.

Outside the museum Volunteer Park was named during the Spanish-American War of 1898 to honour those who had served as soldiers. Climb the water tower for a splendid 360-degree view, or stroll through the graceful Conservatory, where thousands of plants in five separate rooms simulate botanical environments from around the world. In winter, there's nothing like stepping into the tropics room, filled with giant ferns, palms and orchids. Just north of the park boundaries at Lake View Cemetery (► 58), you can pay tribute at the graves of actor and martial arts legend Bruce Lee and his son, Brandon.

Museum of Flight

This stunning building is quite simply the finest air and space museum on the West Coast. Even technophobes will be engaged and delighted.

Flight path The 185,075-sq foot Museum of Flight is on the southwest corner of Boeing Field and King County International Airport, and is partly housed in the original Red Barn, where the Boeing Company built its first planes.

Great Gallery The Red Barn exhibit documents early aviation up to 1938, while the airy and breathtaking Great Gallery traces the story of flight from early mythology to the latest accomplishments in space. Overhead, more than 20 full-sized aeroplanes hang at varying levels from a ceiling grid. All face the same direction, like a squadron frozen in flight. Another exhibit contains artefacts from the Apollo space programme, including an Apollo command module, lunar rocks and the Lunar Roving Vehicle. The museum also has a full-sized air traffic control tower. Like a working tower, this simulated version overlooks airport runways and has overhead speakers that broadcast air traffic transmissions. Outside the museum building, you can tour the original Air Force One presidential jet.

You be the pilot In the fascinating Tower Exhibit, you can pilot an imaginary flight from Denver to Seattle to witness the behind-the-scenes work of air traffic controllers. Through visual cues on a radar screen and telephone instructions, you can perform the numerous tasks required to fly the plane, from checking weather data and filing a flight plan to landing.

HIGHLIGHTS

- A restored 1917 Curtiss 'Jenny' biplane, Charles Lindbergh's first plane
- A flying replica of the B&W, Boeing's first plane
- The only MD-21 Blackbird spy plane in existence
- Apollo space programme artefacts
- A full-sized air traffic control tower
- Piloting an imaginary flight

INFORMATION

- ✚ Off map M3; Locator map B4
- ✉ 9404 E Marginal Way South by Boeing Field (I-5 exit 158)
- ☎ 206/764–5720
- 🕙 Daily 10–5 (Thu to 9PM)
- 🍴 Wings Café, open museum hours
- 🚌 174
- ♿ Excellent
- 💲 Moderate. Free 1st Thu of month, 5–9PM
- ❓ Guided museum tours; lectures, concerts, films and special events

A 1917 Curtiss 'Jenny'

University of Washington

The University campus was originally planned as a fairground for Seattle's 1909 Exposition celebrating the Alaska Gold Rush. Much of the design, including Rainier Vista – a concourse framing Mt Rainier – has been preserved.

DID YOU KNOW?

- Most locals call the university 'U Dub'
- Suzzalo & Allen Library was modeled after King's College Chapel in Cambridge, England
- Husky Stadium has seats for 72,000 people

INFORMATION

- A5/6; Locator map B3
- Between 15th and 25th Avenue, NE and Campus Parkway, and NE 45th Street; (UW Visitor Center, Mon–Fri, 4014 Univeristy Way NE at Campus Parkway)
- 206/543–9198, Visitor Center
- Mon–Fri 8–5
- 70, 71, 72, 73, 43, 25
- Good
- Henry Art Gallery (► 45), Burke Museum (► 46), Arboretum (► 47), Museum of History and Industry (► 52), U District (► 55)

Vistas and fountains Established in 1861 on a site in the downtown area, the university moved to its present location 30 years later. To begin your tour stop at the Visitor Information Center to pick up a free self-guided walking tour map and an events schedule. As you walk, you'll see buildings in a variety of architectural styles, from turreted Denny Hall to cathedral-like Suzzalo & Allen Library. The Suzzalo & Allen faces Red Square, a student gathering place. Only the *Broken Obelisk* sculpture and three campanile towers break the horizontal line of this plaza, which is bordered by Meany Hall, a performing arts venue.

Elsewhere To the west, lies the Henry Art Gallery (► 45). To the north, the old campus quadrangle is especially inviting in late March or early April when rows of pink Japanese cherry trees burst into bloom. Continuing towards the university's north entrance, you come to the Burke Museum (► 46) and UW's observatory, which is open to the public. If you head towards the Waterfront Activities building, you can hire a canoe and paddle on Lake Washington.

The Ave One block west of the campus lies University Avenue Northeast, known as 'the Ave', the main drag through the 'U district'. Here, a multitude of ethnic restaurants, music and bookshops, import shops and second-hand shops share the avenue with street kids who call the neighbourhood 'home'.

Above: part of the university campus. The Cascade Mountains are on the horizon

Henry Art Gallery

The Henry Art Gallery expanded its gallery space in 1997 with an addition that takes advantage of the sloping site and greatly enhances the building. Today, the Henry is Seattle's leading venue for cutting-edge art.

The new Henry Architect Charles Gwathmey's remodel quadrupled the museum's space while managing to preserve its original façade and easterly views over the university campus. The design features a series of windows and skylights that bring natural light into the building.

Installations The Henry encourages experimentation and frequently presents artists whose work is visually and conceptually challenging.

The collection Works from the permanent collection are exhibited on a rotating basis in the old building's North Gallery. A cornerstone of the collection is the Monsen Collection of Photography, prized for its scope, from vintage prints to contemporary explorations of the medium. The permanent collection also includes late 19th- and early 20th-century landscape painting; modern art by Stuart Davis, Robert Motherwell, Jacob Lawrence and Lionel Feininger; examples from the Northwest School; and an extensive Native American textile collection.

Learn as you go In addition to films, lectures and children's events, the gallery also presents Midday Art Moments twice monthly at 2:15PM, when curatorial staff and guests speak about current exhibitions and Art Dialogues, discussions of the current show, held once a month during Thursday's free evening hours. For programme information, check the website: www.henryart.org.

DID YOU KNOW?

● Founded in 1927, the Henry was the first public art museum in the state

HIGHLIGHTS

● The Monsen Collection of Photography
● Regular artists' lectures, symposia and film showings
● Special hands-on workshops for children one Saturday a month

INFORMATION

✚ A5; Locator map B3
✉ UW campus at 15th Avenue. NE and NE 41st Street
☎ 206/543–2280 ; 543–2281 for scheduled tours/events
🕐 Tue–Sun 11–5 (Thu to 8). Closed Mon and 4 July, Thanksgiving, Christmas and New Year
🍴 Gallery café
🚌 70, 71, 72, 73, 43, 25
♿ Very good
💵 Moderate; free Thu 5–8
🔁 University of Washington (► 44), Burke Museum (► 46), Arboretum (► 47), Museum of History and Industry (► 52), U District (► 55)
❓ Tours, lectures and discussions, special events; gallery shop

Burke Museum of Natural History and Culture

The Burke's permanent collection demonstrates at once a keen artistic sense, genuine respect for the cultural traditions of featured groups and a scientist's attention to detail.

The Burke's beginnings The museum's origins date back to 1879, when four enthusiastic teenagers calling themselves the Young Naturalists set about collecting Northwest plant and animal specimens, a popular hobby at the time. Their collection grew, so much that to house it a museum was built on the University of Washington campus in 1885. Over the next 20 years, the number of specimens increased, and today, they form the basis of the Burke's extensive collection, which totals more than three million objects. The museum moved into its current building in 1962.

Treasures on display As you walk through the entrance, a stunning glass display case demands immediate attention. It highlights selected treasures from this vast collection, and gives you an idea of what's in store. In the halls beyond, two new exhibits showcase the museum's strong suits: natural history and ethnography. The Pacific Voices exhibit conveys the variety and richness of Pacific Rim cultures, from New Zealand to the northwest coast of Canada. By framing the exhibit around the celebrations and rituals that are central to each culture, museum artefacts are placed within their appropriate context. Constructed 'sets', photo murals, recorded sounds and informative text bring objects to life and communicate the importance of cultural traditions. The Life and Times of Washington State exhibit is a chronological journey through 545 million years of Washington natural history.

DID YOU KNOW?

- The museum's anthropological division has the largest Northwest Coast collection of Indian artefacts in the western United States
- The 37,000 bird specimens in the ornithology collection account for 95 per cent of North American species
- Before the Burke opened, a number of ethnic groups came to the museum for private 'blessing' ceremonies to consecrate their installations

INFORMATION

- ✚ B6; Locator map B3
- ✉ University of Washington campus at NE 45th Street and 17th Avenue NE
- ☎ 206/543–5590 or 206/543–7907 (exhibit/special events)
- 🕐 Fri–Wed 10–5, Thu 10–8
- 🍴 Burke Café.
- 🚌 70, 71, 72, 73, 43
- ♿ Very good
- 💰 Moderate. 'Dollar Deal': pay an extra dollar for same-day admission to the Henry
- ↔ University of Washington (➤ 44), Arboretum (➤ 47), Museum of History and Industry (➤ 52), U District (➤ 55)

Washington Park Arboretum

This large botanical collection owes its origins to Edmond S Meany, founder of the University of Washington's School of Forestry. Today's garden combines exotics with virtually every woodland plant indigenous to the area.

Green oasis Meany initiated a seed exchange with universities around the world. As a result, you can walk through a variety of ecological zones and enjoy a rich diversity of flora.

The Japanese Garden On the west side of Lake Washington Boulevard, tucked away behind a wooden fence, lies the restful Japanese Garden. Elements of the garden – plants, trees, water, rocks – and their placement, represent a miniature world of mountain, forest, lake, river and tableland. There's also a ceremonial teahouse.

Waterfront trail This 1½-mile trail, originating behind the Museum of History and Industry (▶ 52), winds through marshland on floating platforms and footbridges. At Foster Island, it cuts under the Evergreen Point Floating Bridge and continues through what was once a Native American burial ground to Duck Pond. To experience this convergence of man and nature from the water, hire a canoe (▶ 57) and go for a paddle through water-lilies among the mallards and their ducklings.

DID YOU KNOW?

- Arboretum area: 200 acres
- Botanist Edmond S Meany test-planted imported seeds in his own garden, and later transplanted the plants on campus
- The Japanese Garden was designed in 1960 by Juki Iida, a Tokyo landscape architect, who personally supervised both its planning and construction

INFORMATION

- ✚ B6, C6; Locator map B3
- ✉ Between E Madison Street and Hwy 520, and 26th Avenue E and Arboretum Drive E (Graham Visitor's Center at 2300 Arboretum Drive E)
- ☎ 206/543–8800; Japanese Garden 206/684–4725
- 🕐 Daily 8AM to sunset; Japanese Garden 1 Mar to 30 Nov daily
- 🚌 11
- ♿ None
- 💰 Waterfront and woodland trails free; Japanese Garden free
- 🔄 University of Washington (▶ 44), Museum of History and Industry (▶ 52)
- ❓ Free guided tours at weekends, year-round.

The Boeing Tour

Over the years, Seattle's fortunes have soared and dipped on the wings of Boeing. Touring the 747 plant and seeing workers on the job puts a human face on the region's largest employer.

Ceaseless activity Thirty minutes north of Seattle, in the world's largest building measured by volume, thousands of employees go about the intricate process of assembling wide body jets. Here, 747s, 767s and the newest, the 777, are assembled around the clock.

The tour The 90-minute Boeing tour begins with a short film. Afterwards, a guide takes you to the plant's third floor, where an observation deck provides a view of the final 747 assembly operation. Outside, you are shown where the painting, fuelling and ground testing of the aircraft occurs.

Company history After flying with a barnstorming pilot at a 1915 flight show, young William Boeing was convinced of two things: that he could build a better plane, and that aviation was destined for more than mere entertainment. In 1916 he and naval architect Conrad Westerveld built the B&W, the first Boeing aircraft. Following World War I, the company struggled on the verge of bankruptcy and manufactured furniture to stay afloat. Boeing's boom years commenced with the production of the B-17 bomber. Company fortunes continued to soar through the Cold War until 1969, when recession hit, but again, the company recovered. In 1996, Boeing merged with Rockwell, contractor for the US space shuttle, and in 1997, with McDonnell-Douglas, makers of the DC9. With its divisions spread further afield, Boeing announced in 2001 its plans to move corporate headquarters out of the state. Manufacturing facitities will remain here.

DID YOU KNOW?

- Boeing now owns Rockwell, contractor for the US space shuttle and McDonnell Douglas, manufacturer of the DC9
- Workers use bicycles to traverse the factory floor
- Boeing offers buyers a range of customised interiors. The new 747-400s for Saudi Arabian Airlines provide curtained prayer rooms equipped with electronic devices pointing to Mecca
- The Boeing plant covers 98.3 acres under one roof
- 26 overhead cranes cruise on 31 miles of networked track

INFORMATION

- Off map J3; Locator map C1
- Tour Center off Hwy 189 West (via I-5 northbound)
- 206/544–1264 (recording); 1–800/464–1746
- Summer: Mon–Fri: hourly, 9, 10–3; winter: daily twice or more. Closed weekends. Gray Line of Seattle tours (206/626–5208. Admission guaranteed)
- Very good
- Inexpensive
- Tickets distributed at 8AM for same day tours. Individual admission on first-come basis; gift shop

SEATTLE's
best

Parks & Beaches *50–51*

Museums *52*

Public Art *53*

Architecture *54*

Neighbourhoods *55*

Active Pursuits *56–57*

What's Free & Nearly Free *58*

Free Events *59*

For Children *60*

Parks & Beaches

THE GREEN CITY

The city's 300 or so parks are often cited as key to Seattle's liveability. Credit goes to city officials, who feared that unchecked logging would destroy Seattle's natural beauty, and to Chicago's Olmsted Brothers Landscape Architects, who were hired to draft a comprehensive plan for the city in 1903. The system of parks and connecting boulevards they designed forms the backbone of Seattle's 5,000 acres of parkland.

In the Top 25

2 ALKI BEACH (► 25)
1 DISCOVERY PARK & DAYBREAK STAR ART CENTER (► 24)
3 THE HIRAM M CHITTENDEN LOCKS (► 26)
19 VOLUNTEER PARK (► 42)
24 WASHINGTON PARK ARBORETUM (► 47)
5 WOODLAND PARK ZOO (► 28)
See Evening Strolls for
GREEN LAKE (► 18)
MYRTLE EDWARDS/ELLIOTT BAY PARK (► 18)

FREEWAY PARK

When Freeway Park opened in 1976, it won national attention for the ingenious way it created an urban oasis over ten lanes of freeway. The design called for a concrete 'lid' to go over Interstate 5, pollution-resistant trees and a waterfall thundering at a rate of 27,000 gallons a minute to mask the traffic noise. Note George Tsutakawa's handsome bronze fountain.

✚ F6 ✉ 6th Avenue and Seneca Street, south of Washington State Convention Center 🚌 2

GASWORKS PARK

This park on north Lake Union is popular for picnics, kite-flying and skateboarding, with it's wonderful views of downtown. Rusted, graffiti-marked towers and brightly painted machinery in the play area recall this site's origins as a gas plant. Climb the grassy mound to see the park's sundial or to launch a kite.

✚ B3 ✉ N Northlake Way and Meridian Avenue N 🚌 26

GOLDEN GARDENS BEACH PARK

This beach park is teen heaven: you'll find a half-mile strip of sandy beach and trail, views of the Olympics, a bathhouse, concessions, picnic shelters and firepits. And if yachts are your thing, check out the ones next door, at Shilshole Marina. A walk along the beach at dusk is a must.

✚ Off map K2 ✉ Seaview Ave 🚌 17

Gasworks Park

KERRY VIEWPOINT

This tiny park on Queen Anne Hill has a great view of downtown and features Doris Chase's steel sculpture *Changing Form*.

➕ C2 ✉ W Highland Drive and 2nd W 🚌 2 or 13

LINCOLN PARK

In this lovely West Seattle park south of Alki, you'll find something for everyone: great views, rocky beaches with tidepools, walking and biking trails, picnic shelters, tennis courts, a horseshoe pit, a children's playground and Seattle's only outdoor saltwater pool and waterslide.

➕ Off map M2 ✉ Fauntleroy Avenue SW and SW Webster 🚌 54

MADISON PARK

In this neighbourhood beach park on the western shore of Lake Washington, you can sunbathe on a grassy slope. There's a bathhouse and a swimming dock with diving board. Lifeguards operate throughout the summer.

➕ C6 ✉ The foot of E Madison Street at 43rd Avenue E 🚌 11

MATTHEWS BEACH

At this swimming beach on the north shore of Lake Washington, bikers on the 16½ mile lakeside Burke-Gilman trail stop to cool down or enjoy a picnic on the grassy meadows. There's also a playground for the children.

➕ Off map K3 ✉ NE 93rd off Sand Point Way NE 🚌 75

SEWARD PARK

This beautiful 277-acre wilderness on the south shore of Lake Washington has a beach and trails along the waterfront and through old-growth cedar and fir forest (where it is sometimes possible to catch views of the two pairs of nesting eagles). It's a wonderful place for a picnic, especially if you come via bicycle on a Bicycle Saturday or Sunday, when Lake Washington is closed to traffic. Also features a fish hatchery and picnic shelters with barbecues.

➕ Off map L3 ✉ Lake Washington Boulevard S and S Juneau 🚌 39

SEATTLE AREA BEACHES

With several freshwater lakes and miles of shoreline along Elliott Bay, Seattle boasts a number of beach parks within its city limits. However, in Seattle the term 'beach' is not necessarily synonymous with 'swimming'. Few choose to swim in the chilly waters of Puget Sound, apart from a quick dash in and out on a hot summer's day. The freshwater of Greenlake and Lake Washington, on the other hand, are pleasant for more extended swims.

Golden Gardens Beach Park, backed by the snow-capped Olympic Mountains

Eastside Museums

In the Top 25

23 BURKE MUSEUM OF NATURAL HISTORY & CULTURE (► 46)

9 EXPERIENCE MUSIC PROJECT ► 31)

22 HENRY ART GALLERY (► 45)

16 KLONDIKE GOLD RUSH NATIONAL HISTORIC PARK (► 39)

20 MUSEUM OF FLIGHT (► 43)

6 PACIFIC SCIENCE CENTER (► 29)

13 SEATTLE ART MUSEUM (► 36)

18 SEATTLE ASIAN ART MUSEUM (► 42)

15 WING LUKE MUSEUM (► 41)

BELLEVUE ART MUSEUM (BAM)

In a new building designed by architect Steven Holl, BAM has no permanent collection. The building's sculptural properties and use of natural light embody its mission of going beyond exhibition to both exploring and generating art.

- ✉ 510 Bellevue Way NE
- ☎ 425/519–0770; www.bellevueart.org
- 🕐 Tue–Wed, Fri–Sat, 10–5; Thur 10–8; Sun 12–5. Closed holidays
- 🚌 550 from bus tunnel
- 💲 Moderate

FRYE ART MUSEUM

This beautiful, spacious gallery devoted to representational art rotates works from the permanent collection, most notably pieces by William Merritt Chase, Winslow Homer, John Singer Sargeant and Renoir.

➕ E4 ✉ 704 Terry Avenue ☎ 206/622–9250 🕐 Tue–Sat 10–5; Thur till 9; Sun noon–5 🍴 Café on site 🚌 3, 4 (on 3rd Avenue) 🎵 Sun afternoon concerts ⚑ Excellent 💲 Free

An old salmon advertisement, Museum of History and Industry

MUSEUM OF HISTORY AND INDUSTRY (MOHAI)

Two new exhibits have made this small museum a lively learning centre: Salmon Stakes brings the early canning industry to life; in Seattle Roots you assume a pioneer identity and follow your character along a 19th century Seattle street.

➕ B5 ✉ 2700 24th Avenue E, south of the Montlake Bridge ☎ 206/324–1126 🕐 Daily 10–5; closed Thanksgiving, Christmas, New Year and Mon except holiday Mondays 🚌 25, 43, 48, 255 ⚑ Excellent 💲 Moderate

NORDIC HERITAGE MUSEUM

This is the only museum in the United States to showcase the heritage of all five Nordic nations: Denmark, Finland, Iceland, Norway and Sweden. In the Dream of America exhibit you follow the immigrant experience: departure, crossing, a new land and the industries in which immigrants played important roles, especially logging and fishing. Five other galleries tell the unique story of each Nordic group. The museum also presents excellent contemporary art exhibitions and cultural events.

➕ G1 ✉ 3014 NW 67th Street ☎ 206/789–5707 🕐 Tue–Sat, 10–4; Sun noon–5 🚌 17 (on 4th Avenue) 💲 Inexpensive; free first Tue of month

Public Art

┌─ See elsewhere for ─────────────────────┐
ADJACENT, AGAINST, UPON (➤ 18)
21 BROKEN OBELISK (➤ 44)
2 DAYBREAK STAR ART CENTER (➤ 25)
GASWORKS SUNDIAL (➤ 50)
13 HAMMERING MAN (➤ 36)
└───┘

A SOUND GARDEN
One of Seattle's small treasures. Doug Hollis's ingenious work consists of 12 steel towers supporting wind activated organ pipes that create gentle sounds on windy days.
➕ C4 ✉ Behind NOAA building, 7600 Standpoint Way NE
🚌 74, 75

DANCERS' SERIES: STEPS
At each of eight locations, Jack Mackie has fashioned cast bronze shoeprints in the pattern of a couple's feet as they dance the tango, waltz, lindy, foxtrot, rhumba and mambo.
✉ Broadway on Capitol Hill 🚌 7

FREMONT TROLL
This whimsical giant, who is crushing a real Volkswagen Bug with his bare hand, is both a reference to Scandinavian folklore and an expression of Fremont's collective sense of humour.
➕ A3 ✉ N 36th Street under the Aurora Avenue Bridge 🚌 26, 28

OCCIDENTAL PARK TOTEMS
Duane Pasco's painted cedar logs – *Sun and Raven*, *Tsonqua* and *Killer Whale and Bear* – date from 1975.
➕ G6 ✉ Occidental Park, Occidental Avenue S and S Main in Pioneer Square 🚌 Buses on 1st in free zone

RAIN FOREST GATES
Artists Jean Whitesavage and Nick Lyle depict plant and animal forms of the NW rainforest in these forged steel gates at the corner of 2nd and South Jackson.
🚌 7, 14, 36

WAITING FOR THE INTERURBAN
Richard Beyer's sculpture is a much-loved fixture of Fremont. Rarely are these gray aluminium trolley riders unadorned, either with scarves and hats in winter, or at other times through the year with balloons and banners to acknowledge someone's birthday.
➕ A3 ✉ Fremont Avenue N and N 34th Street
🚌 26, 28

PUBLIC ART
From manhole covers and benches to bus tunnel tiles, public art is incorporated into the very fabric of Seattle's daily life. Artists worked with architects and engineers on the design for five underground stations: Convention Place, Westlake, University, Pioneer Square and the International District. The design reflects the character of each neighbourhood. This art phenonemon stems from the city's May 1973 'One Percent for Art' ordinance, which specifies that 1 per cent of all new municipal improvement funds must be set aside for the purchase and installation of public art. At least half of all allocations are awarded to artists residing in the Pacific Northwest. After an open call for applications selection is finalised following a review by a Seattle Arts Commission panel.

The troll at Fremont

Architecture

In the Top 25

1 DAYBREAK STAR ART CENTER (➤ 24)
8 EXPERIENCE MUSIC PROJECT (➤ 31)
23 HENRY ART GALLERY (➤ 45)
20 MUSEUM OF FLIGHT (➤ 43)
6 PACIFIC SCIENCE CENTER (➤ 29)
13 SEATTLE ART MUSEUM (➤ 36)

CHAPEL OF ST IGNATIUS

This sublime chapel is Seattle University's architectural gift to the city. Architect Steven Holl visualized the structure as 'seven bottles of light in a stone box', with light bouncing off the tinted baffles to create a halo effect on surrounding walls.
➕ E4 ✉ 12th Avenue near Marion on Capitol Hill 🕐 Mon–Thu 7AM–10PM; Fri 7–7; Sat 9–5; Sun 9–11. Regular liturgies ☎ 206/296–6075 🚌 2, 12

The ornate interior of the Fifth Avenue Theater

FIFTH AVENUE THEATER

Built in 1926, this ornately carved theater is patterned after the imperial throne room in Beijing's Forbidden City.
➕ F6 ✉ 1308 5th Avenue ☎ 206/625–1900 🚌 Downtown free zone buses along 1st to 4th Avenue

HARBOR STEPS

In creating a pedestrian link between the Waterfront and 1st Avenue Vancouver architect Arthur Anderson crafted an inviting urban plaza with waterfalls, seating and plantings.
➕ F6 ✉ University Avenue 🚌 Downtown free zone buses along 1st to 4th Avenue

SMITH TOWER

When it opened in 1914, Smith Tower was Seattle's first steel-framed skyscraper and the tallest building outside of New York City. At 42 storeys, it remained the tallest building west of the Mississippi until 1969. For a modest fee, you can ride to the 35th floor in the company of the last of Seattle's lift attendants to get a sweeping view of downtown.
✉   506 2nd Avenue and Yesler Way

SECURITY PACIFIC BANK TOWER

Architect Minoru Yamasaki once said that he tried to create 'delight, serenity and surprise' in his buildings. This inverted white pencil, balanced on a 12-storey base, clearly succeeds at least on the last count.
➕ F6 ✉ 1200 4th Avenue between Union and University 🚌 Downtown free zone buses along 1st to 4th Avenue

WASHINGTON MUTUAL BUILDING

As critics lambasted this late 1980s Kohn Pederson Fox building as an Empire State clone, the public applauded the post-modern style as relief from the cold glass boxes that dominate downtown.
➕ F6 ✉ 1201 3rd Avenue 🚌 Downtown free zone buses along 1st to 4th Avenue

Neighbourhoods

In the Top 25
---

2 ALKI BEACH (➤ 25)
15 DOWNTOWN (➤ 38)
18 THE INTERNATIONAL DISTRICT (➤ 41)
14 LAKE UNION (➤ 37)
16 PIONEER SQUARE (➤ 39)
9 THE WATERFRONT & AQUARIUM (➤ 32)

BELLTOWN

This unconventional neighbourhood north of the
Market is an odd mix of seediness and gentrification.
The area's working-class roots are still evident even
as upmarket restaurants and condos, cyber-cafés and
taverns with art on the walls have transformed and
energised the neighbourhood.
🚌 Buses on 1st and 3rd

CAPITOL HILL

Diverse and progressive, two miles east of downtown,
Capitol Hill is the focal point of the Seattle gay
community, and home to a smattering of Seattle's
monied elite as well as young professionals and
seniors on fixed incomes. The action is concentrated
along Broadway in cafés, restaurants, retro shops
and clubs.
🚌 7 to Broadway E, or 10 to 15th Avenue E

FREMONT

This offbeat neighbourhood, which proclaims itself a
republic and 'the Center of the Universe', is known
for its tolerance and quirky humour. Check out the
public art, from the monumental statue of Lenin
to the Volkswagen-crushing *Fremont Troll* under
Aurora Bridge.
🚌 26, 28

MADISON PARK

This older residential neighbourhood
bordering Lake Washington at the foot
of Madison boasts lovely homes, a
popular beach (➤ 51) and a cluster of
interesting speciality shops and cafés.
🚌 11 to the foot of Madison

UNIVERSITY DISTRICT

This area includes the University of Washington
(➤ 44), 'the Ave', and University Village, a complex
of tasteful speciality shops, markets and cafés.
'The Ave' is full of student haunts and the
awesome and justifiably renowned University
Bookstore.
🚌 Many including 7, 43, 70, 71,72, 73, 85

FREMONT FOLLIES

Seattle has earned its 'most
liveable city' moniker through
the strength and character of
its neighbourhoods, of which
Fremont, where tongue-in-
cheek irreverence runs high,
ranks as the quirkiest. In
Fremont, bumper-stickers that
elsewhere in the United States
read: 'HONK IF YOU LOVE
JESUS'; instead ask you to:
'HONK IF YOU *ARE* JESUS'.

*Artistic graffiti in
Fremont*

55

Active Pursuits

┌─── **See Evening Strolls for** ──────────────────┐
│ **GREEN LAKE (▶ 18)**
│ **MYRTLE EDWARDS/ELLIOTT BAY PARK (▶ 18)**
│ **See Parks and Beaches for**
│ **MADISON PARK, MATTHEWS BEACH, SEWARD**
│ **PARK (▶ 51)**
└──┘

SEATTLE BY BIKE

Despite the omnipresent threat of drizzle and the challenge of hilly terrain, growing numbers of Seattleites are taking to two wheels for commuting and recreation. The city is laced with bike trails, including a number of flat, scenic routes that reward bikers and in-line skaters with spectacular views.

BIKE TRAILS

• Alki Beach to Lincoln Park: This bikeway is marked only part of the way; continue along the shoreline to Lincoln Park for a 12-mile round trip. (Flat.)
🚌 37 (daytime only), 56

• Burke-Gilman Trail: This 16½ mile, paved, lakeside trail follows an old railway right-of-way, skirting Fremont, Wallingford and the University of Washington campus. From Fremont/Ballard, the trail runs east along the ship canal, Lake Union and Portage Bay. At the University of Washington's Husky Stadium, the trail swings north along Lake Washington and continues for 12 miles to the northern tip of the lake at Kenmore. If you want to go to the Woodinville Wineries and Brewpub, pick up the Sammamish River Trail. (Flat.)

• Lake Washington Boulevard. In summer on Bicycle Saturdays and Sundays, traffic is barred from a 6-mile stretch of Lake Washington Boulevard, between the arboretum and Lake Washington and south along the lake to Seward Park. (Mostly flat; one hill.) This part joins Seward Park's 2½ mile loop. (▶ 51)

Exploring Seattle by bike

☎ Bicycle Sat/Sun Schedule: 206/684-4075

• Magnolia Bluff Bike Trail: Three miles from Discovery Park to Magnolia Park with views of Elliott Bay, the Olympics, West Seattle, Mt Rainier and downtown. (Moderate, one steep hill.)
🚌 24, 33

BIKE HIRE

• Blazing Saddles. Downtown shop features a ride wall and detailed bike ride directions.
➕ F5 ✉ 1230 Western Avenue at bottom of harbor steps
☎ 206/341–9994; www.blazingsaddles.com 🕐 Daily 9AM
🛏 Reasonable rates with discounts for hostellers

• Gregg's Green Lake Cycle. In-line skates for hire.
➕ A6 ✉ 7007 Woodlawn Avenue NE ☎ 206/523–1822

• Magnolia Alpine Hut: bikes, in-line skates and sit-on kayaks for hire in summer; skis in winter.
🚏 B1 ✉ 2215 15th Avenue W ☎ 206/284–3575 🕐 Mon–Fri 10–6; Sat 10–5; Sun in winter: noon–5 🚌 15, 18
• Montlake Bicycle Shop
🚏 C5 ✉ 2223 24th Avenue E (near the Arboretum) ☎ 206/329–7333 🚌 43

BOAT HIRE

• Agua Verde Paddle Club: hourly kayak hire from its boat-house and tasty, economical Mexican eats and drinks up above.
🚏 A4 ✉ 1303 NE Boat Street (on Portage Bay) ☎ 206/545–8570
• Green Lake Boat Rentals: paddleboats and rowing boats.
🚏 A6 ✉ 7351 E Green Lake Drive N ☎ 206/527–0171 🕐 May to autumn 🚌 26
• On Lake Washington/Portage Bay: UW Waterfront Activities Center: canoes.
🚏 A4 ✉ Waterfront Activities Building ☎ 206/543–9433 🚌 25, 43
• On Lake Union: Center for Wooden Boats: sailboats and rowing boats.
🚏 B3 ✉ 1010 Valley Street ☎ 206/382–2628 🕐 May–Oct: daily 11–7. Nov–Apr: daily 11–5 🚌 17
• Moss Bay Rowing and Kayak Center: kayaks and shells – hire, lessons, tours.
🚏 C4 ✉ 1001 Fairview Avenue N #1900 ☎ 206/682–2031 🚌 70, 71, 72, 73
• Northwest Marine Charters, 26 feet plus, sails and power; one-day skippered outings.
🚏 B3 ✉ 2400 Westlake N ☎ 206/283–3040 🚌 17
• NW Outdoor Center: kayaks, also classes, day trips.
🚏 B3 ✉ 1500 Westlake Avenue N ☎ 206/281–9694 🚌 17
• Wind Works Sailing Center. Bare boat or skippered charters.
🚏 G1 ✉ 7001 Seaview NW, Suite 133 ☎ 206/784–9386; www.sail/1.com 🕐 Open year-round

FISHING

• A Spot Tail Salmon Guide: Salmon fishing in Puget Sound with guide and gear provided.
🚏 Off map ✉ 2318 Viewmont Way W ☎ 206/283–6680 🚌 19, 24
• Seacrest Boat House: aluminium boats for hire with motor and bait; half or full day.
🚏 F1 ✉ 1660 Harbor SW ☎ 206/932–1050 🚌 37

GOLF

Seattle has three 18-hole public golf courses.
• Jackson Park
🚏 Off map K3 ✉ NE 135th and 10th Avenue NE, off I-5 ☎ 206/363–4747 🚌 73
• Jefferson Park
🚏 G4 ✉ 4101 Beacon Avenue S ☎ 206/762–9949 🚌 36
• West Seattle Golf Course
🚏 Off map L2 ✉ 4470 35th SW ☎ 206/935–5187 🚌 21, 22,

Canoeing on Lake Union

THE BURKE-GILMAN TRAIL: HIGHLIGHTS

- Fremont neighbourhood
- Gasworks Park
- University of Washington campus
- University Village
- Sound Garden public art (near by)
- Matthews Beach (extension to Sammamish River Trail)
- Woodinville Wineries
- Redhook Brewery, Woodinville

What's Free & Nearly Free

FREE ADMISSION DAYS

Many of Seattle's museums and other attractions have free or cheap admission days once a month. Here's a selection:

- First Tuesday of the month: Nordic Heritage Museum; the Children's Museum ('pay as you can' 5–8 PM)
- First Thursday of the month: Seattle Art Museum; Seattle Asian Art Museum
- First Thursday of the month, 5–8 PM: Pioneer Square Gallery Walk; Museum of Flight
- Every Thursday: Henry Art Gallery (5–8 PM)
- First Saturday of the month: Seattle Asian Art Museum

Seattle Asian Art Museum

┌─ In the Top 25 ─────────────────

1 DISCOVERY PARK & DAYBREAK STAR ART CENTER (➤ 24)
11 FERRY TO BAINBRIDGE ISLAND (➤ 34)
4 FISHERMEN'S TERMINAL (➤ 27)
10 KLONDIKE GOLD RUSH NATIONAL HISTORIC PARK(➤ 39)
3 THE HIRAM M CHITTENDEN LOCKS (➤ 26)
10 PIKE PLACE MARKET (➤ 33)
17 REI (➤ 40)
18 VOLUNTEER PARK (➤ 42)

COAST GUARD MUSEUM

On pier 36, the museum features a collection of navigational aids, ships models and various maritime artefacts explaining the history and work of the Coast Guard.

➕ F3 ✉ Pier 36 on waterfront ☎ 206/217–6993 🕐 Mon, Wed, Fri, 9–3; Sat–Sun 1–5

GLASS-BLOWING DEMONSTRATIONS

• Edge of Glass Gallery: Here at his studio and shop in Fremont, John Walsh creates glass art.

➕ A3 ✉ 513 N 36th Street #H ☎ 206/547–6551 🕐 Wed–Sun 11–6 🚌 26, 28

• Glasshouse Art Glass, Ltd: Watch glass-blowers at work in this Pioneer Square studio to the large gallery.

➕ G6 ✉ 311 Occidental Avenue S ☎ 206/682–9939 🕐 Mon–Sat 10–3; Sun 11–3 🚌 Any buses on 1st (free zone)

HISTORY HOUSE

Depicts the history of Seattle neighbourhoods with photo displays, interactive kiosks and animated slide shows. Also features a small sculpture garden.

➕ A2 ✉ 790 N 34th Street in Fremont ☎ 206/675–8875 🕐 Wed–Sun 11–5

LAKE VIEW CEMETERY

Seattle's pioneers are buried here, but it's the graves of martial arts cult star Bruce Lee (near the top of the hill) and his son, Brandon, that draw visitors.

➕ C4, C5 ✉ 1554 15th Avenue East at E Garfield on Capitol Hill 🚌 10

VOLUNTEER PARK WATER TOWER

Best free view of the city.

➕ C4, C5 ✉ West of 15th Avenue E between E Prospect and E Galer 🚌 10

WOODLAND PARK ROSE GARDEN

This test garden with over 5,000 roses normally peaks in early July.

➕ Off map ✉ 5500 Phinney Avenue N 🚌 5 (from 3rd and Pine)

Free Events

BREWERY TOURS
• Pike Place Brewery has a microbrew museum.
➕ F5 ✉ 1415 1st Avenue ☎ 206/622–3373 🕐 Daily 11–11
🚇 Downtown free zone
• Pyramid Breweries. Daily tours, with samples of
Pyramid Ales and Thomas Kemper lagers and sodas.
➕ A5 ✉ 1201 1st Avenue S ☎ 206/682–3377 🚇 Downtown
free zone
• Redhook Ale Brewery: The first in Seattle with
craft brews. Daily tours at two locations, one in
Fremont and the other at Woodinville, 25 minutes
northeast of Seattle.
➕ Off map ✉ 3400 Phinney Avenue N ☎ 206/548–8000
🚌 26, 28
✉ Woodinville ☎ 425/483-3232

ELLIOTT BAY BOOK COMPANY READINGS
This first-rate independent bookshop, great to browse,
has a café and a programme of readings by noted
authors six days a week, usually for free. Arrive early.
➕ G6 ✉ 101 S Main Street ☎ 206/624–6600 for ticket
information 🚇 Downtown free zone

FREMONT SUNDAY MARKETS
Fresh produce, flowers and crafts.
➕ A3 ✉ Fremont neighborhood around N 34th and Evanston Avenue
🕐 May–Oct: Sun 10–4

FRYE MUSEUM CONCERTS
Classical music concerts on Sunday afternoons.
➕ E4 ✉ 704 Terry Avenue ☎ 206/622–9250 🚌 3, 4, 12

OUT TO LUNCH WEEKDAY CONCERTS
Midday concerts through the summer at various
downtown locations.
🕐 Jun–Sep Mon–Fri ☎ 206/623–0340 for information.

UNIVERSITY DISTRICT FARMERS' MARKET
Flowers and farm fresh produce, summer Saturdays.
➕ A6 ✉ University Way NE and NE 50th 🚌 70, 71, 72, 73, 43

WINERIES
• Chateau Ste. Michelle. Daily tours and tastings
10–4:30; summer concerts.
➕ Off map K3 ✉ 14111 NE 145th Street in Woodinville, NE of Seattle
☎ 425/488–3300 🚌 255 to Kingsgate (exit at NE 143rd and 131
Avenue NE. Walk east on NE 143rd, which becomes NE 145th, for 0.8 miles)
• Columbia Winery: One of Washington's pioneer
wineries.
✉ 14030 NE 145th ☎ 425/488–2776
• Bainbridge Island Winery: A small family vineyard
and winery. Tastings and picnic area. Under a mile
north of the ferry dock on Bainbridge Island.

HANDMADE BREWS

Seattles brewers have
pioneered the US's move
away from mass-produced
beers to more subtly flavoured
'craft brews'. With at least
eight brewpubs in the area,
some call Seattle 'the
microbrew capital of the
world'.

For Children

Cooling off Seattle-style

In the Top 25

㉓ BURKE MUSEUM (► 46)
⑪ FERRY TO BAINBRIDGE ISLAND (► 34)
⑭ LAKE UNION (► 37)
⑳ MUSEUM OF FLIGHT (► 43)
❻ PACIFIC SCIENCE CENTER (► 29)
⑰ REI (► 40)
❾ THE WATERFRONT & AQUARIUM (► 32)
❺ WOODLAND PARK ZOO (► 28)

CHILDREN'S MUSEUM

Activities focus on the arts and humanities. Children can write their own cartoons and then watch their characters spring to life; build fanciful crafts in artist-led workshops; and enter the time tunnel to ancient Greece.
➕ D2 ✉ The Center House, first level, Seattle Center ☎ 206/441–1768 ⏰ Mon–Fri 10–5; Sat–Sun 10–6. Jun–Sep: Mon–Fri 10–6; Sat–Sun 10–7. Closed holidays 🚌 3, 4, 16, 24, 33 to Seattle Center

FUN FOREST AMUSEMENT PARK

Rides, carnival games and candyfloss.
➕ D3 ✉ Seattle Center ☎ 206/728–1585 ⏰ Jun–Aug: noon–11. Off season hours vary 🚌 3, 4, 16 to Seattle Center

NW PUPPET CENTER

Multicultural stories from around the world. Productions by the award-winning Carter Family Marionettes, the resident company and by guest companies from all over the globe. Theatre includes small exhibit area. Seven different productions, Oct–May and summer tours.
➕ A5 ✉ 9123 15th Avenue NE ☎ 206/523–2579; www.nwpuppet.org 🚌 73, 77, 78

ODYSSEY MARITIME DISCOVERY CENTER

Three state-of-the-art exhibits highlight the working waterfront: you can board a 'virtual kayak' and negotiate the Puget Sound inlets, while Harvesting the Sea gives you the opportunity to skipper a commercial fishing boat, and the Ocean Trade gallery allows you to load a container vessel and measure yourself against the pros.
➕ D3 ✉ Bell Harbor's Pier 66 ☎ 206/374–4000
🚋 Waterfront streetcar

SEATTLE CHILDREN'S THEATER

Recognised worldwide for its innovative programming. With over 20 seasons under its belt and the fanciful new Charlotte Martin Theater, SCT is a prized cultural resource for families.
➕ D2 ✉ Seattle Center ☎ 206/441–3322 ⏰ Season Sep to Jun 🚌 1, 2, 3, 4, 16, 24, 33 to Seattle Center

A GREAT PLACE FOR CHILDREN

In the 1980's, Seattle launched a major effort to create a more 'child-friendly' urban environment that would discourage the exodus of middle class families to the suburbs. The city joined forces with civic groups to create an abundance of outdoor recreation and entertainment venues.

SEATTLE
where to...

EAT
Northwest Classics &
  American Cuisine *62–63*
Seafood & Vegetarian *64–65*
Asian/Sushi *66*
Mexican/Nuevo–Latino *67*
Romantic/Bistro Dining *68*
Coffee Shops &
  Breakfast Bests *69*

SHOP
Men's & Women's
  Clothing *70-72*
Art & Antiques *73*
Books, CDs & Tapes *74*
Gifts *75*
Speciality Shops *76*
Kitsch, Funk & Retro *77*

BE ENTERTAINED
Theatre & Film *78*
Classical Music, Dance
  & Opera *79*

Rock, Jazz & Blues Venues *80*
Other Venues & Hang-outs *81*
Bars, Pubs & Taverns *82*
Spectator Sports *83*

STAY
Luxury Hotels *84*
Mid-Range Hotels *85*
Budget Accommodation *86*

Northwest Classics
& American Cuisine

PRICES

Expect to pay per person for a meal, excluding drinks:

£ = Under $15
££ = $15 to $30
£££ = over $30

NORTHWEST CLASSICS

CAMPAGNE (£££)

Award-winning country-French fare in the heart of the Pike Place Market featuring one of the city's best wine lists.

✚ F5 ✉ 86 Pine Street
☎ 206/728–2800 🕔 Dinner nightly

CANLIS (£££)

Excellent Northwest fare with Asian accents. The restaurant's been a special occasion destination for more than 50 years.

✚ A3 ✉ 2576 Aurora Avenue N ☎ 206/283–3313
🕔 Dinner Mon–Sat

DAHLIA LOUNGE (££)

Innovative Northwest cuisine in lively, colourful surroundings.

✚ E6 ✉ 2001 4th Avenue
☎ 206/682–4142
🕔 Weekday lunch, dinner nightly

FULLERS (£££)

The Sheraton Hotel is home to this famously innovative Northwest cuisine restaurant.

✚ E6 ✉ 1400 6th Avenue
☎ 206/447–5544
🕔 Breakfast, lunch and dinner Tue–Sat

LE GOURMAND (£££)

For more than two decades this nondescript, hard-to-find French-Northwest spot has been making locals swoon.

✚ G1 ✉ 425 NW Market Street ☎ 206/784–3463
🕔 Dinner Wed–Sat

THE HERBFARM (£££)

Think ahead if you want to eat at this legendary, award-winning restaurant serving seasonal Northwest cuisine: extremely popular.

✚ Off map ✉ 14590 NE 145th Street (at Willows Lodge)
☎ 206/784–2222
🕔 Reservations required

THE METROPOLITAN GRILL (£££)

Stellar steaks and legendary martinis draw crowds nightly. Happy hour features inexpensive food specials in the bar, where stogies are encouraged.

✚ F6 ✉ 820 2nd Avenue
☎ 206/624–3287 🕔 Lunch on weekdays, dinner nightly

THE PAINTED TABLE (££)

Fresh produce taken from the Pike Place Market is transformed into artful Northwest cuisine at this longtime Seattle landmark.

✚ F5 ✉ 92 Madison Street
☎ 206/624–3646 🕔 Breakfast, lunch and dinner daily

PALISADE (£££)

Polynesian cocktails, an indoor fish pond with a footbridge, and a view of Puget Sound and sailboats moored outside make this a popular special occasion destination.

✚ D2 ✉ 2601 W Marina Place ☎ 206/285–1000
🕔 Weekday lunch, dinner nightly, weekend brunch

ROVER'S (£££)

Often credited with serving the first haute cuisine in Seattle, the menu is full of truffles and *fois gras*.

✚ C6 ✉ 2808 E Madison Street ☎ 206/325–7442
🕔 Dinner Tue–Sat

SALISH LODGE RESTAURANT (£££)

Perched above Snoqualmie Falls, the cozy interiors of the restaurant offer stunning views and the menu features artful Northwest fare.

Off map ✉ 6501 Railroad Avenue SE, Snoqualmie ☎ 800/826–6124 Breakfast, lunch, dinner, brunch at weekends

SKYCITY AT THE NEEDLE (£££)

Five hundred feet above Seattle, the pricey dinners are only average, but the view is priceless.

D3 ✉ 219 4th Avenue N (in the Space Needle) ☎ 206/443–2111 Lunch, dinner and weekend brunch

SZMANIA'S (££)

This once ground-breaking restaurant is now a neighbourhood spot filled with loyal regulars.

E6 ✉ 3321 W McGraw Street ☎ 206/284–7305 Dinner Tue–Sat

AMERICAN CUISINE

5 SPOT (£)

An ever-changing menu that concentrates on different regions every few months: You never know if you'll get Creole catfish or New England clam chowder.

B2 ✉ 1502 Queen Anne Avenue N ☎ 206/285–7768 Breakfast, lunch, dinner and brunch

HATTIE'S HAT (£)

One of Seattle's oldest and proudest diners pours a stiff drink and cooks up some mean comfort food.

Off map ✉ 5231 Ballard Avenue NW ☎ 206/784–0175 Dinner nightly, weekend brunch

HILLTOP ALE HOUSE (£)

This neighbourhood eatery is great for catching a game and does better-than-pub grub with a variety of microbrews on tap.

C2 ✉ 2129 Queen Anne Avenue N ☎ 206/285–3877 Lunch and dinner daily

PALACE KITCHEN (££)

Urban American dining at its best. High-ceilings and dim lighting make the gas station, uniform-clad cooks in the open kitchen even more fun to watch.

E5 ✉ 2030 5th Avenue S ☎ 206/448–2001 Weekday lunch, dinner nightly

RED MILL BURGERS (£)

Truly great burgers, shakes and onion rings. Kid-friendly, but it's such a great place to eat that it's usually packed with adults.

G2 ✉ 312 N 67th Street ☎ 206/783–6362 Lunch and dinner Tue–Sun

SIX ARMS (£)

Microbrews on tap and tasty burgers and fries in a laid-back, comfortable, neighbourhood pub that also has spacious wooden booths.

E6 ✉ 300 E Pike Street ☎ 206/223–1698 Lunch and dinner daily

COMMON MEALS CAFÉ (£)

This non-profit restaurant serves delicious, hearty meals at budget prices while training homeless men and women for jobs in the food service industry. The weekday lunch buffet, which includes a range of remarkably ambitious preparations, is popular and on Thursday nights, top chefs from local restaurants prepare outstanding dinners. There's a fixed price for full-course meals and all proceeds are ploughed back into the programme.

E5 ✉ 1902 2nd Avenue Lunch Mon–Fri 11–2, dinner Thu only ☎ 206/439–5361

Seafood & Vegetarian

SEAFOOD

ANTHONY'S HOMEPORT RESTAURANTS (££)

Airy and attractive restaurants each afford fine waterfront views and fresh seafood, salads and desserts. Full bar.
➕ D3 ✉ Pier 66, 2201 Alaskan Way, on the waterfront ☎ 206/448–6688
▣ Waterfront trolley
➕ G1 ✉ At Shilshloe in Ballard, 6135 Seaview NW ☎ 206/783–0780 ▭ 46

BROOKLYN SEAFOOD, STEAK & OYSTER BAR (££)

The perfect place for slurping cool oysters and sipping ice-cool martinis.
➕ F5 ✉ 1212 2nd Avenue ☎ 206/224–7000 ⏰ Lunch on weekdays, dinner nightly

THE CRAB POT (££)

The waterfront location and come-as-you-are appeal is perfect for families. Don a bib and crack your crab right on the paper-lined tables.
➕ D3 ✉ 1301 Alaskan Way (Pier 57) ☎ 206/624–1890 ⏰ Lunch and dinner daily

CUTTERS (£££)

Family-friendly seafood dining at the north end of Pike Place Market.
➕ D3 ✉ 2001 Western Avenue ☎ 206/448–4884 ⏰ Lunch and dinner daily; brunch Sunday

ETTA'S SEAFOOD (££)

Located just outside of Pike Place Market, Seattle restaurateur Tom Douglas' ode to seafood with an Asian, innovative bent is a favourite with the crowds.
➕ E5 ✉ 2020 Western Avenue ☎ 206/443–6000 ⏰ Lunch and dinner daily; brunch at weekends

FLYING FISH (££)

Hip, stylish, approachable and always packed. Expect unusual fish and fun preparation. Don't miss the family-style fish tacos.
➕ E5 ✉ 2234 1st Avenue ☎ 206/728–8595 ⏰ Dinner daily

IVAR'S (£)

Ask anyone for fish'n' chips in Seattle and they'll send you to Ivar's. The casual fish bars are ideal for an easy lunch.
➕ D3 ✉ 1001 Alaskan Way ☎ 206/624–6852 ⏰ Lunch and dinner daily

JACK'S FISH SPOT (£)

Locals know this is the place to go for great cioppino and fresh fish 'n' chips.
➕ E3 ✉ 1514 Pike Place ☎ 206/467–0514 ⏰ Lunch daily

PALISADE (£££)

Seafood with Polynesian flare and a stunning waterfront location make this place a special occasion must.
➕ Off map ✉ 2601 W Marine Place ☎ 206/285–1000 ⏰ Lunch and dinner daily; brunch at weekends

RAY'S BOATHOUSE (£££)

A to-die-for view and dependably good seafood are the draws at this lively fish house. The upstairs café offers a waterside outdoor deck and plenty of people-watching.
➕ G1 ✉ 6049 Seaview Avenue NW ☎ 206/789–3770 ⏰ Lunch and dinner

RESTAURANT ZOE (££)

Set in the heart of Seattle's hip Belltown neighbourhood, young, beautiful and discerning diners pack the room for expertly prepared fish and seafood, and fun cocktails.
➕ E5 ✉ 2137 2nd Avenue ☎ 206/256–2060 ⏰ Dinner Mon–Sat

SALTY'S ON ALKI (££–£££)

There's simply no better view of the stunning Seattle skyline. Features approachable seafood preparations and a famous Sunday brunch.

➕ Off map ✉ 1936 Harbor Avenue SW ☎ 206/937–1600 🕐 Lunch, dinner and brunch

THIRD FLOOR FISH CAFÉ (£££)

Set three floors above the shores of Lake Washington in Kirkland, this upmarket fish house offers some of the best seafood around.

➕ Off map ✉ 205 Lake Street, Kirkland ☎ 425/822–3553 🕐 Dinner nightly

WATERFRONT (£££)

Asian-accented fine dining worthy of locals and tourists alike on the breathtaking shores of Lake Union. The outdoor, waterside seating is the best place in town for sunset gazing.

➕ D2 ✉ 2801 Alaskan Way (Pier 70) ☎ 206/956–9171 🕐 Dinner nightly

VEGETARIAN

CAFÉ AMBROSIA (£££)

Upmarket, all-organic vegan cuisine on the shores of Lake Union.

➕ B4 ✉ 2501 Fairview Avenue E ☎ 206/325–7111 🕐 Dinner nightly, brunch on Sun

CAFÉ FLORA (££)

A glass-lined atrium dining room sets the stage for harmonious meat-free fare. Sunday brunches are very popular here so call and make a reservation.

➕ F6 ✉ 2901 Madison Street ☎ 206/325–9100 🕐 Lunch and dinner daily, brunch on weekends

CARMELITA (££)

Creative and innovative dining set in the charming Phinney Ridge neighbourhood. Outdoor seating is available.

➕ A2 ✉ 7314 Greenwood Avenue N ☎ 206/706–7703 🕐 Dinner only, closed Mon

FLOWERS (£)

Funky, laid-back college bar with a terrific vegetarian lunch buffet.

➕ A6 ✉ 4247 University Way NE ☎ 206/633–1903 🕐 Lunch and dinner daily

GRAVITY BAR (£)

Menu consists of mostly vegan dishes and the friendly staff will amend non-vegan dishes to suit. .

➕ D4 ✉ 415 Broadway E ☎ 206/325–7186 🕐 Sun–Thu 10–10; Fri–Sat 10–11

GREEN CAT CAFÉ (£)

Urban vegetarian coffee shop with terrific daily specials and tasty morning fare.

➕ D4 ✉ 1514 E Olive Way ☎ 206/726–8756 🕐 Breakfast, lunch and dinner daily

STILL LIFE (£)

A living room of artsy folks sipping coffee and noshing on veg-friendly vittles.

➕ A2 ✉ 709 N 35th Street ☎ 206/547–9850 🕐 Breakfast, lunch and dinner daily

Asian/Sushi

SUSHI

SANMI SUSHI (££)
This tiny, unassuming eatery next to Palisades on Magnolia's Smith Cove has, some say, the best sushi in town. Beer, wine, sake.
➕ D2 ✉ 2601 Marina Place ☎ 206/283-9978 🍴 Closed Sat–Sun lunch 🚌 19, 24

DRAGONFISH ASIAN CAFÉ (££)
A fun eatery with lively appetisers and speciality martinis in the heart of the hotel district.
➕ E6 ✉ 722 Pine Street ☎ 206/467-7777 🍴 Lunch and dinner daily

KAU KAU BARBECUE (£)
Addictive roast duck and barbecued pork. Take it to go, since ambience is lacking.
➕ E4 ✉ 656 S King Street ☎ 206/682-4006 🍴 Lunch and dinner daily

KRITTIKA NOODLES AND THAI (£)
Crowds line up for the terrific Thai at this spot in the heart of the Green Lake neighbourhood.
➕ Off map ✉ 6411 Latona Avenue NE ☎ 206/985-1182 🍴 Lunch on weekdays, dinner nightly

KWANJAI THAI (£)
A neighbourhood favourite with some of the best green curry in the city.
➕ A3 ✉ 469 N 36th Street ☎ 206/632-3656 🍴 Lunch and dinner daily

I LOVE SUSHI (££)
Popular, crowded sushi bar on the shores of Lake Union.
➕ B4 ✉ 1001 Fairview Avenue ☎ 206/625-9604 🍴 Lunch on weekdays, dinner nightly

MALAY SATAY HUT (£)
Authentic Malaysian food that has locals lining up nightly for a daring taste of something different.
➕ F4 ✉ 200 12th Avenue S ☎ 206/324-4091 🍴 Lunch and dinner daily

NISHINO (££)
Impeccable sushi and terrific *omakase* (chef-designed prix-fixe dinners) in upmarket, soothing surroundings.
➕ F6 ✉ 3130 Madison Street ☎ 206/322-5800 🍴 Dinner nightly

SHANGHAI GARDEN CHINESE RESTAURANT (££)
An endless menu featuring fresh seafood and exotic ingredients in the heart of the International District.
➕ E4 ✉ 524 6th Avenue S ☎ 206/625-1689 🍴 Lunch and dinner daily

SHIRO'S SUSHI (££)
Immaculate sushi served in a crisp setting. Sit at the bar for the ultimate experience.
➕ D3 ✉ 2401 2nd Avenue ☎ 206/443-9844 🍴 Dinner nightly

WASABI BISTRO (££)
Hip clientele enjoy Americanised sushi rolls and a variety of Japanese dishes at this popular spot in the heart of Belltown.
➕ D3 ✉ 2311 2nd Avenue ☎ 206/441-6044 🍴 Dinner nightly

WILD GINGER (££)
The most popular and perhaps most lauded restaurant in Seattle serving legendary Fragrant Duck, with a bar that's bulging with beautiful people.
➕ F6 ✉ 1401 3rd Avenue ☎ 206/623-4450 🍴 Dinner nightly

Mexican/Nuevo-Latino

EL CAMINO (££)

Lively crowds pack this Fremont neighbourhood spot for Mexican fare and tasty margaritas.

➕ A3 ✉ 607 N 35th Street ☎ 206/632–7303 🕑 Dinner daily. Closed Labor Day

FANDANGO (££)

Upmarket Mexican with polish. The bar attracts well-dressed 30-somethings for *tapas* and cocktails.

➕ G3 ✉ 2313 1st Avenue ☎ 206/441–1188 🕑 Dinner nightly

HARVEST VINE (££)

A tiny neighbourhood best-kept-secret with some of the best *tapas* in the city and a queue every night.

➕ F6 ✉ 2701 Madison Street ☎ 206/320–9771 🕑 Dinner Tue–Sat

MAMA'S MEXICAN KITCHEN (££)

The funky crowds of Belltown head here for inexpensive American-Mexican fare and sip cocktails amid the kitschy decor.

➕ D3 ✉ 2234 2nd Avenue ☎ 206/728–6262 🕑 Lunch and dinner nightly

TANGO TAPAS RESTAURANT & LOUNGE (££)

Stylish dining on the edge of Seattle's Capitol Hill neighbourhood. Great *mojitos* and a large selection of tequilas make for a lively bar.

➕ E6 ✉ 1100 Pike Street ☎ 206/583–0382 🕑 Weekday lunch, dinner nightly

ITALIAN & PIZZA

2ND AVE PIZZA (£)

An urban pizzaria that's open late and shows old films in the back room on weekends.

➕ E5 ✉ 2015 2nd Avenue ☎ 206/956–0489 🕑 Weekday lunch, dinner Mon–Sat

ASSAGGIO (££)

Lively, spirited and always packed. Pastas are terrific, but can be bested by daily specials.

➕ E5 ✉ 2010 4th Avenue ☎ 206/441–1399 🕑 Weekday lunch, dinner Mon–Sat

CAFÉ JUANITA (£££)

A perennial favourite that just keeps getting better, this quiet Kirkland spot is worth the drive from Seattle.

➕ Off map ✉ 9702 NE 120th Place, Kirkland ☎ 425/823–1505 🕑 Dinner Tue–Sun

IL TERRAZZO CARMINE (£££)

A Seattle institution worthy of its reputation. Some of the best Italian food in the city awaits.

➕ F3 ✉ 411 1st Avenue S ☎ 206/467–7797 🕑 Weekday lunch, dinner Mon–Sat

MACHIAVELLI (££)

Casual, inexpensive and tasty pastas served on tables laid with chequered tablecloths, perfect for dates or groups of friends.

➕ E6 ✉ 1215 Pine Street ☎ 206/621–7941 🕑 Dinner Mon–Sat

Romantic/Bistro Dining

AVENUE ONE (£££)

Sit outside under an umbrella or in one of the plush booths and enjoy French bistro fare featuring Northwest produce. The restaurant also boasts an award-winning wine list.

✚ E5 ✉ 1921 1st Avenue ☎ 206/441–6139 🕐 Dinner nightly

CAFÉ CAMPAGNE (££)

Dim and warm, this cosy spot in the Pike Place Market is perfect for a glass of wine. Sunday brunch is one of the best in the city.

✚ F5 ✉ 1600 Post Alley ☎ 206/728–2233 🕐 Breakfast, lunch and dinner daily

CAFÉ NOLA (££)

Hop on a ferry to Bainbridge Island and escape to the tidy tidings of this eclectic island eatery.

✚ Off map ✉ 101 Winslow Way, Bainbridge Island ☎ 206/842–3822 🕐 Dinner daily, lunch weekdays

CASSIS (££)

Warm, inviting and intimate, this French bistro offers satisfying fare to flocks of loyal patrons.

✚ B4 ✉ 2359 10th Avenue E ☎ 206/329–0580 🕐 Dinner nightly

CHEZ SHEA (££)

An outstanding view from this delightful bistro with flower-topped white-linen tables make for romance in the Market.

✚ F5 ✉ 94 Pike Street ☎ 206/467–9990 🕐 Dinner Tue–Sun

LA FONTANA (££)

An urban romantic oasis filled with candlelight, and named for the trickling fountain in the courtyard.

✚ E5 ✉ 120 Blanchard Street ☎ 206/441–1045 🕐 Dinner Mon–Sat

LE PICHET (££)

Café au lait in the morning, baguette sandwiches at lunch and charcuterie and ever-changing specials at night make for casual French café dining at its best.

✚ E5 ✉ 1933 1st Avenue ☎ 206/256–1499 🕐 Breakfast daily, lunch and dinner Thu–Mon

LUSH LIFE (££)

It's easy to walk right by this hidden Italian spot without noticing, but it's a true find for a romantic dinner or drink. Mostly traditional dishes served.

✚ E5 ✉ 2331 2nd Avenue ☎ 206/441–9842 🕐 Dinner nightly

MISTRAL (£££)

Exquisite prix-fixe dining in a calm, quiet respite in the heart of bustling Belltown.

✚ E5 ✉ 113 Blanchard Street ☎ 206/770–7799 🕐 Dinner Tue–Sat

SERAFINA (££)

Rustic Italian by candlelight and an outdoor deck to enjoy a summer evening.

✚ B4 ✉ 2043 Eastlake Avenue E ☎ 206/323–0807 🕐 Dinner daily, lunch weekdays

Coffee Shops & Breakfast Bests

611 SUPREME (£)
Crepes and French press coffee in a charming Capitol Hill spot.
✚ E6 ✉ 611 E Pine Street ☎ 206/382–02927 🕔 Tue–Sun dinner, weekend brunch

BAUHAUS (£)
Stylish coffee bar and bookshop offering choice people-watching and selling Ding Dongs.
✚ E6 ✉ 301 E Pine Street ☎ 206/625–1600 🕔 Breakfast and lunch daily

B & O ESPRESSO (£)
Coffee and a wide selection of desserts in one of Seattle's classic espresso bars.
✚ D4 ✉ 204 Belmont Avenue E ☎ 206/322–5208 🕔 Breakfast, lunch and dinner daily

CAFÉ SEPTIEME (£)
Coffee and other diversions served with attitude to hipsters on Broadway.
✚ D4 ✉ 214 Broadway E ☎ 206/860–8858 🕔 daily

CAFFE LADRO (£)
Adirondack chairs line the front of this friendly Queen Anne neighbourhood coffee shop.
✚ A3 ✉ 2205 Queen Anne Avenue N ☎ 206/282–5313

ESPRESSO VIVACE (£)
The best place to get a cup of coffee in the city, with umbrella-shaded tables that are perfect for people-watching.
✚ D4 ✉ 321 Broadway E ☎ 206/860–5869 🕔 Open daily

GLO'S (£)
Start the day with one of the homely breakfasts served at this charming diner-like spot on Capitol Hill.
✚ E6 ✉ 1621 E Olive Way ☎ 206/324–2577 🕔 Breakfast daily

LUX COFFEE BAR (£)
Hip coffee-break and lunch spot with fresh-air appeal in the heart of Belltown.
✚ E5 ✉ 2226 1st Avenue ☎ 206/443–0962 🕔 Lunch daily

MACRINA BAKERY (£)
Freshly baked breads and pastries, and shots of espresso greet sleepy urbanites in the early hours. Freshly prepared daily 'special' sandwiches and soups continue to draw crowds as the day wears on.
✚ E5 ✉ 2408 1st Avenue ☎ 206/448–4032 🕔 Breakfast, lunch and dinner daily

TEAHOUSE KUAN YIN (£)
A quiet respite from the bustle of the city offering every imaginable sort of tea.
✚ A3 ✉ 1911 N 45th Street ☎ 206/632–2055 🕔 Open daily

UPTOWN ESPRESSO (£)
This neighbourhood coffee shop makes a great place to sit and sup a perfect latte, or a cappuccino with boast-worthy foam.
✚ A3 ✉ 525 Queen Anne Avenue N ☎ 206/285–3757 🕔 Open daily

BAGELS

BAGEL OASIS (£)
Delicious bagels with a variety of spreads. Several locations including:
Fremont ✚ A2 ✉ 462 N 36th 🕔 26, 28
Downtown ✚ F6 ✉ 4th and Seneca 🕔 Closed dinner

SEATTLE BAGEL BAKERY (£)
First-rate bagels. Order 'to go' for a picnic outside, on the Harbor Steps.
✚ F5 ✉ 1302 Western Avenue ☎ 206/624–2187

Men's & Women's Clothing

SHOPPING DISTRICTS

Seattle's finest clothing shops tend to be clustered in several neighbourhoods: The Downtown retail core between Stewart and Pike (N–S) and 3rd and 6th avenues includes: Bon Marche (3rd and Pine), Nordstrom's (5th and Pine), City Center (1420 5th Avenue) Westlake Mall (4th and Pine). Nearby is: Rainier Square (bounded by 4th and 5th Avenues and University–Union streets.). Other areas: Belltown (1st and 2nd from Bell Street) Broadway East on Capital Hill.

CASUAL WEAR/ OUTDOOR APPAREL

ADERCROMBIE & FITCH
Well-made clothes for well-heeled men and women.
➕ A6 ✉ 2540 NE University Village ☎ 206/729–3510

BANANA REPUBLIC
Casual clothes in natural fibres.
➕ E6 ✉ 500 Pike Street in Coliseum Bldg ☎ 206/622–2303

EDDIE BAUER
Casual wear and accessories for men and women with an outdoor lifestyle.
➕ F6 ✉ 1330 5th Avenue across from Rainier Square ☎ 206/622–2766 ⏰ Mon–Fri 10–8; Sat 10–7; Sun 11–6

THE GAP
Yes, the Gap. Essential stop for young men and women's casual coordinates. Open daily at four locations.
✉ Downtown at 1530 5th Avenue ☎ 206/625–1470); ✉ Capitol Hill in the Broadway Market, ☎ 206/325–3852; ✉ 2730 NE University Village ☎ 206/525–1559 ✉ Northgate Mall ☎ 206/361–0305

J CREW
Stylish, casual wear for men and women with the emphasis on natural fibres and comfort.
➕ E6 ✉ 600 Pine Street, Pacific Place (also at Bellevue Square) ☎ 206/652–9788

PATAGONIA
State-of-the-art outdoor clothing for adults and children.
➕ E5 ✉ 2100 1st Avenue ☎ 206/ 622–9700

REI
Outdoor clothing and gear runs the gamut from hiking equipment to bikes, kayaks and nature books.
➕ D4 ✉ 222 Yale Avenue N ☎ 206/223–1944

WARSHAL'S
Sporting goods emporium of the 'Army & Navy Store' genre with a large selection of hunting, fishing and camping equipment, plus outdoor clothing, boots and a photo department.
➕ F6 ✉ 1000 1st Avenue ☎ 206/624–7300 ⏰ Closed Sun

FASHION (BY NEIGHBOURHOOD)

DOWNTOWN CITY CENTRE

ANN TAYLOR
Classic lines and easy elegance in women's fashions ranging from career to informal wear.
➕ E3 ✉ Pacific Place, City Center and University Village ☎ 206/623–4818

APRIL CORNELL
Feminine styles and charming, colourful prints for women and young girls.
➕ D3 ✉ Westlake Center ☎ 206/749–9658

BARNEYS
Chic and trendy for that minimalist New York style. Prada and other popular designers. Shoes, jewellery, accessories and skin products.
➕ F6 ✉ 1420 5th Avenue in City Center ☎ 206/622–6300

BCBG
Beautiful evening gowns,
career and casual creations
by Paris designer Max Azria.
✚ E6 ✉ 600 Pine Street,
Pacific Place ☎ 206/447–3400

BETSEY JOHNSON
For adventuresome and
young-at-heart women
who like fun and flam-
boyance in their clothing.
✚ F6 ✉ 1429 5th Avenue
☎ 206/624–2887

BROOKS BROTHERS
Superior men's clothing in
traditional styles.
✚ F6 ✉ 1335 5th Avenue
☎ 206/624–4400

BUTCH BLUM
Expensive European-styled
men's apparel from famous
designers' exclusive
collections, as well as more
original, avant-garde lines.
✚ F6 ✉ 1408 5th Avenue
☎ 206/622–5760 ⏰ Closed
Sun

CHICOS
Distinctive and fun
women's clothes with
attitude that travel easily.
Mostly wash and wear.
✚ E6 ✉ 600 Pine Street,
Pacific Place ☎ 206/624–5549

DAVID LAWRENCE
Stylish European men's
fashion from Hugo Boss,
Donna Karan, Versace and
more. Suits to sportswear.
Professional tailoring.
✚ D3 ✉ 4th Avenue at Union
☎ 206/622–2544

EILEEN FISHER
Simple yet elegant apparel
for the professional
woman of 30 or 65.
✚ E6 ✉ 525 Pine Street at
6th Avenue ☎ 206/748–0770

HELEN'S (OF COURSE)
Exclusive fashions for
women over 50 with haute
couture from Oscar de la
Renta and other designers.
✚ F6 ✉ 1302 5th Avenue
☎ 206/624–4000
⏰ Closed Sun

KENNETH COLE
This prominent designer
opened a Seattle shop in
November 2000 featuring
chic styles for today's men
and women.
✚ E5 ✉ 520 Pike Street
☎ 206/298–0007

MARIO'S
Fashionable downtown
clothing shop specialising
in clean, classic lines and
featuring designers like
Donna Karan and Giorgio
Armani. Also shoes and
accessories.
✚ E6 ✉ 1513 6th Avenue
☎ 206/223–1461

NORDSTROM
This venerable institution
stocks clothing for the
entire family.
✚ E5 ✉ 500 Pine Street. Also
at Bellevue Square and Northgate
Mall. ☎ 206/628–2111

NUBIAS
Relaxed sophistication for
women in styles that
reflect owner-designer
Nubia's Latin roots with
accents from Asia.
✚ E6 ✉ 1507 6th Avenue and
4116 E Madison in Madison Park
☎ 206/622 0297 🚌 11

TOTALLY MICHAEL'S
Sophisticated women's
clothing for work, play and
after dark.
✚ F6 ✉ 521 Union Street
☎ 206/622–4920
⏰ Closed Sun

SEATTLE AREA SHOPPING MALLS

Bellevue Square
This suburban mall on the east
side of Lake has a vast array of
high-end clothing and
speciality shops, department
stores and eateries.
✉ NE 8th Street and Bellevue
Way NE. ⏰ Mon-Sat
9:30–9:30; Sun 11–7
🚌 Downtown to Eastside
over SR520 floating bridge.

University Village
With an upscale renovation
begining in 1995, U Village
now includes branches of a
number of major players in
the retail market.
✉ NE 45th and 25th Avenue
NE, east of the University of
Washington campus
⏰ Mon-Sat 9:30–9; Sun 11–6
🚌 From downtown

Northgate Mall
The first enclosed mall in the
United States, Northgate
opened in 1950. Renovated in
the late 1990's, the mall
includes four department
stores, an assortment of small
shops and a food court.
✉ I5 north to 110th NE
(Northgate Way) ⏰ Mon-Sat
10–9:30; Sun 11–6 🚌 Express
service from downtown to
Northgate station

SIZE CONVERSION

A = America
B = Britain
F = France
I = Italy
E = Rest of Europe

Women's clothes

A	8	10	12	14	16
B	10	12	14	16	18
F	38	40	42	46	48
I	40	42	44	46	48
E	36	38	40	42	44

Men's shirts

A	14½	15	15½	16	16½
B	14½	15	15½	16	16½
E	37	38	39/40	41	42

Shoes

A	5½	6½	7½	8½	9½	10½	11½
B	4	5	6	7	8	9	11
E	36	38	39	40	41	42	44

BELLTOWN (ALONG 1ST AVENUE)

BABY & CO
Pricey, whimsical clothes for adventurous women.
✚ E5 ✉ 1936 1st Avenue
☎ 206/448–4077

C P SHADES
Casually sophisticated natural fibre women's clothing – dresses, trousers, skirts, vests and tunics made of cotton, silky rayon and velvet; deep, subtle hues.
✚ E5 ✉ 2025 1st Avenue #A
☎ 206/448–9218

DAKOTA
Classic women's clothes and accessories by American designers.
✚ E5 ✉ 2025 1st Avenue
☎ 206/441–3177

DARBURY STENDERU
Stunning wearable art for women with hand-painted designs; beautiful colours and fabrics.
✚ E5 ✉ 2121 1st Avenue
☎ 206/448–2625
Ⓒ Closed Sun

DITA BOUTIQUE
Unusual selections of women's wear for all ages; range includes many imports.
✚ F5 ✉ 1525 1st Avenue, #2
☎ 206/622–1770

ENDLESS KNOT
Elegant and original women's clothes.
✚ E5 ✉ 2232 1st Avenue
☎ 206/448–0355

OPUS 204
Custom designed women's clothing, jewellery and accessories – simple, yet sophisticated lines in beautiful fabrics. Antiques and collectables are sold here also.
✚ E5 ✉ 2004 1st Avenue
☎ 206/728–7707 🚌 7

CAPITOL HILL (ALONG BROADWAY)

URBAN OUTFITTERS
New and vintage clothing popular with the young and trendy; also sells housewares, jewellery, gifts. In the Broadway Market.
✚ D4 ✉ 401 Broadway E
☎ 206/322–1800 🚌 7

YAZDI'S
Dresses, skirts, vests and softly draping pants for women – made of rayon and cotton in beautiful Indonesian prints.
✚ D4 ✉ 401 Broadway E
☎ 206/860–7109 🚌 7
Other stores in Pike Place Market and Wallingford Center

PIONEER SQUARE

DESIGN PRODUCTS CLOTHING
Distinctive women's clothing from casual to tailored, including evening wear. Local designer Deliane Klein is well represented.
✚ F3 ✉ 208 1st Avenue S
☎ 206/624–7795

FLYING SHUTTLE
Eye-catching hand-woven women's clothing and wearable art; handpainted silk purses and scarves complemented by the exquisite jewellery.
✚ G6 ✉ 607 1st Avenue in Pioneer Square
☎ 206/343–9762

Art & Antiques

AZUMA GALLERY
Japanese art including old and new prints, paintings, screens, folk art and ceramics.
⊕ G6 ✉ 530 1st Avenue S
☎ 206/622–5599
🕐 Tue–Sat 11–6

FLURY & CO GALLERY
Vintage photographs of Native American life; Native American artefacts, beadwork and carvings.
⊕ F3 ✉ 322 1st Avenue S
☎ 206/587–0260

FOSTER-WHITE GALLERY
Work by Pilchuk Glass artists like Dale Chihuly and other prominent artists.
⊕ G6 ✉ 123 S Jackson
☎ 206/622–2833
🕐 Mon–Sat 10–5:30; Sun noon–5

FRANCINE SEDERS GALLERY
In addition to famous names like Jacob Lawrence and Michael Spafford, Seders represents a growing number of minority artists.
⊕ Off map ✉ 6701 Greenwood Avenue N (west of Greenlake) ☎ 206/782–0355
🕐 Tue–Sat 11–5; Sat 1–5

G GIBSON GALLERY
Photographs and related fine art including works by notable Northwest artists like Marsha Burns.
⊕ G6 ✉ 122 S Jackson, Suite 200 ☎ 206/587–4033
🕐 Tue–Fri 11–5:30; Sat 11–5

GREG KUCERA GALLERY
A top city gallery.
⊕ G6 ✉ 212 3rd Avenue S.
☎ 206/624–0770;
www.gregkucera.com
🕐 Tue–Sat 10:30–5:30

HONEYCHURCH ANTIQUES
The foremost shop for fine Asian antiques, especially Japanese and Chinese.
⊕ E4 ✉ 1008 James Street
☎ 206/622–1225
🕐 Tue–Sat 11–5

THE LEGACY
Seattle's oldest and finest gallery for Northwest Native American and Inuit art and artefacts. Founded in 1933.
⊕ G6 ✉ 1003 1st Avenue
☎ 206/624–6350
🕐 Closed Sun

NORTHWEST GALLERY OF FINE WOODWORKING
Local artists' cooperative that exhibits phenomenal craftsmanship and design.
⊕ G6 ✉ 101 S. Jackson
☎ 206/625–0542 🕐 Mon–Sat 10:30–5:30; Sun noon–5

STONINGTON GALLERY
Works by native Northwest Coast master artists Joe David, Robert Davidson, Bill Holm, Duane Pasco and by owner Nancy Stonington.
⊕ E5 ✉ 119 S Jackson
☎ 206/405–4040,
www.stoningtongallery.com
🕐 Mon–Fri 10–6; Sat 10–5:30; Sun noon–5

WILLIAM TRAVER GALLERY
Contemporary painting, sculpture and ceramics by major artists. The gallery is also a leading dealer in contemporary studio glass.
⊕ F5 ✉ 110 Union, 2nd floor
☎ 206/587–6501;
www.travergallery.com
🕐 Mon–Fri 10–6; Sat 10–5; Sun noon–5

ART AND ANTIQUES

FIRST THURSDAY GALLERY WALKS
On the first Thursday of the month, Pioneer Square galleries and those in the Pike Market area open into the evening for the monthly art walk. Many galleries take this opportunity to preview their new shows.

THE PILCHUCK SCHOOL
The Seattle area is well-known for its glass art, primarily through the work of Dale Chihuly and others connected to the world-class Pilchuck Glass School, 50 miles north of Seattle. Examples of Chihuly's work include the large, entry-wall chandeliers at Benaroye Hall and several pieces on display at City Center shopping arcade.

Books, CDs & Tapes

THE INDEPENDENT BOOKSELLER

Seattle has a number of excellent independent booksellers who are committed to bringing quality literature to the public, both blockbusters and smaller works appealing to a more specialised audience. With the arrival of national chains and their well-appointed superstores, independents are feeling the pinch.

ALL FOR KIDS BOOKS AND MUSIC

A wide selection of children's books, music and books-on-tape. Some adult books.

➕ Off map ✉ 2900 NE Blakely Street (behind University Village) ☎ 206/526–2768 🚍 25 🕐 Mon–Sat 10–6; Sun noon–5

BAILEY-COY BOOKS

Well-stocked bookshop with a good selection of gay and lesbian titles.

➕ D4 ✉ 414 Broadway E ☎ 206/323–8842 🚍 7

BUD'S JAZZ RECORDS

Jazz on LP, CD or video.

➕ G6 ✉ 102 S Jackson in Pioneer Square ☎ 206/628–0445

EAST-WEST BOOKSHOP

One of the region's largest stocks of New Age books.

➕ A6 ✉ 1032 NE 65th Street ☎ 206/523–3726 🚍 48, 66

ELLIOTT BAY BOOK COMPANY

More than 130,000 titles, frequent readings and a café in this Pioneer Square haunt.

➕ G6 ✉ 101 S Main Street ☎ 206/624–6600

FREMONT PLACE BOOK COMPANY

This small, cheerful shop features contemporary fiction, Northwest authors, gay and lesbian literature and children's books.

➕ A2 ✉ 621 N 35th Street ☎ 206/547–5970

SECOND STORY BOOKS

Small shop on the 2nd floor of Wallingford Center with an excellent choice of titles.

➕ Off map at A4 ✉ 1815 N 45th ☎ 206/547–4605 🚍 16

SHOREY'S BOOKSTORE

This antiquarian bookseller, which dates back to 1890, is a Seattle treasure in its own right. With an exhaustive number of titles from old paperbacks to rare prints, it is now one of the largest stores of its kind.

➕ A3 ✉ 1109 N 36th Street ☎ 206/633–2990; www.shoreybooks.com/shorey

SILVER PLATTERS

With its huge selection of over 6,000 CDs, this is *the* place to locate that hard-to-find title.

➕ A4 ✉ 9650 1st Avenue NE (near Northgate Mall) ☎ 206/524–3472 🕐 Mon–Sat 10–10; Sun 11–7

TOWER BOOKS

Excellent bookshop that stays open until late.

➕ C3 ✉ 20 Mercer Street ☎ 206/283–6333 🕐 Daily till midnight

TOWER RECORDS

An awesome variety of music for every taste. An in-store Ticketmaster sells tickets to concerts.

➕ A6 ✉ 4321 University Way NE ☎ 206/632–1187 🚍 71, 72, 73, 43

TWICE-SOLD TALES

Wonderful second-hand bookshop.

➕ D4 ✉ 905 E John Street ☎ 206/324–2421 🚍 7, 43

UNIVERSITY BOOKSTORE

One of the nation's largest university bookstores. Also sells art and office supplies, gifts and CDs.

➕ D5 ✉ 4326 University Way NE ☎ 206/634–3400 🚍 71, 72, 73, 43

Gifts

CALDWELL'S
Wonderful imports including folk art, textiles, jewellery and gift items from Central and South America, Africa and Asia.
➕ A6 ✉ 2646 University Village NE ☎ 206/522-7531 🕐 Mon–Sat 9:30–9; Sun 11–6 🚌 25

CRACKERJACK CONTEMPORARY CRAFTS
Unique handcrafted items – many by local artists.
➕ Off map at A4 ✉ 1815 N 45th Street (Wallingford Center) ☎ 206/ 547–4983 🚌 16

DESIGN CONCERN
Everything from desk accessories and housewares to jewellery, with one thing in common: great design.
➕ F6 ✉ 1420 5th Avenue (City Center) ☎ 206/623–4444

FIREWORKS FINE CRAFTS GALLERY
Where crafts meet art, for the playful, the beautiful and unique. Three locations:
➕ G6 ✉ 210 1st Avenue S ☎ 206/682–8707
➕ E6 ✉ Westlake Center ☎ 206/682–6462
➕ A6 ✉ University Village Mall ☎ 206/527–2858

KOBO
Objects with a distinctive Japanese flavour.
➕ C3 ✉ 814 E Roy Street on Capitol Hill ☎ 206/726–0704 🕐 Daily noon–7

LA TIENDA FOLK ART GALLERY
Handcrafted folk art, textiles, women's apparel and musical instruments.
➕ A6 ✉ 4138 University Way NE ☎ 206/632–1796 🕐 Closed Mon 🚌 71, 72, 73, 43

MADE IN WASHINGTON
Handcrafts, foods and wines from the region. Shipping available.
➕ E6 ✉ 400 Pine Street, suite 114, Westlake Center ☎ 206/623–9753
➕ F5 ✉ Pike Place Market and other locations

THE MUSEUM COMPANY
Gifts from jewellery to games and toys. All items are either reproductions or representations of items from museum collections held around the country.
➕ E6 ✉ 600 Pine Street, Pacific Place, suite 225 ☎ 206/342–9294 🕐 Mon–Sat 9:30–8; Sun 11–6

PHOENIX RISING GALLERY
Fine crafts gallery in the north end of the Market showcasing beautiful and original jewellery, ceramics and glassware.
➕ F5 ✉ 2030 Western Avenue in the Pike Place Market ☎ 206/728–2332 🕐 Mon–Sat 10–6; Sun noon–5

PORTAGE BAY GOODS
Environmentally friendly gifts by local and world-wide artisans.
➕ B3 ✉ 706 N 34th ☎ 206/547–5221 🕐 Mon–Sat 10–7; Sun 11–6

UZURI
A potpourri of ethnic gifts, many from Africa, including jewellery, carvings, baskets and clothing.
➕ D4 ✉ 401 Broadway East (in the Broadway Market) ☎ 206/323–3238 🕐 Mon–Fri 10–9; Sat 10–10; Sun noon–7

TASTES OF SEATTLE

What better way to elicit the flavour of the region than to take back a salmon and a bottle of Washington wine. Fishsellers at the Pike Place Market will pack fresh salmon on ice to travel and many fish markets and gift shops like 'Made in Washington' carry gift boxes of smoked salmon that do not require refrigeration. (Also available from port Chatham Packing Co, ☎ 206/781–07260).

Speciality Shops

UWAJIMAYA

In 1928, Fujimatsu Moriguchi began a small business in Tacoma, Washington selling fishcakes from the back of his truck to Japanese loggers and fishermen. He named the business after the Japanese town where he had learned his trade. After World War II, the family moved to Seattle and opened their first retail shop in Seattle's international district. Today, Uwajimaya is the largest gift and grocery store in the Pacific Northwest. A new Uwajimaya Village opened in late 2000, one block south of its former site. The expanded emporium includes several other on-site businesses including Kinokuniya Bookstore, the largest Japanese bookstore chain in the United States, and an Asian food court. Cooking classes offered.
✉ 600 5th Avenue S at Dearborn ☎ 206/624–6248

FACERE JEWELRY ART

Unusual Victorian and contemporary jewellery.
✚ F6 ✉ 1420 5th Avenue in City Center ☎ 206/624–6768

FOX'S GEM SHOP

Fine jewellery since 1912. Expensive.
✚ F6 ✉ 1341 5th Avenue ☎ 206/623–2528 ⓒ Open Mon–Fri 10–6, Sat 10–5:30

FRANK AND DUNYA

Fun, functional and fine arts and crafts by local artists.
✚ A2 ✉ 3418 Fremont Avenue N ☎ 206/547–6760 ⓒ Sun–Mon 10–6; Fri–Sat 10–7

IMPRESS RUBBER STAMPS

Thousands of rubber stamps, pads and papers.
✚ E6 ✉ 400 Pine Street in Westlake Center (also in University Village) ☎ 206/621–1878

LARK IN THE MORNING

Beautiful handmade musical instruments. In Pike Place Market.
✚ E5 ✉ 1411 1st Avenue ☎ 206/623–3440

MAGIC MOUSE

Fanciful, high-end toys for kids of all ages, including stuffed animals, wind-up toys and Brio trains.
✚ E5 ✉ 603 1st Avenue ☎ 206/682–8097

MARKET MAGIC SHOP

Supplies for budding young magicians to pros.
✚ F5 ✉ 1st level below the food stalls, Pike Place Market ☎ 206/624–4271

METZKER MAPS

A wonderful selection of maps of the region and the rest of the world.
✚ E5 ✉ 702 1st Avenue ⓒ Mon–Fri 9–6; Sat 10–5

THE SHARPER IMAGE

State-of-the-art gadgets.
✚ E6 ✉ 1501 4th Avenue, Suite 116 ☎ 206/343–9125 ⓒ Mon–Sat 10–6; Sun 11–5

SOMETHING SILVER

All manner of jewellery, charms, money clips and keychains made of sterling silver.
✚ A6 ✉ 2662 NE University Village ☎ 206/523–7545

THREE DOG BAKERY

Items for that precious pooch, from a vest-style carrier for small pets to 'bark and fetch' biscuits in apple cinnamon, barbeque, peanut butter and carob chip flavours.
✚ E5 ✉ 1408 1st Avenue ☎ 206/364–9999

TRAVELERS

An unusual collection of items from jewellery and textiles, to Shiva lunchboxes and incense.
✚ E5 ✉ 501 E Pine Street ☎ 206/329–6260

UNDERCOVER QUILTS

A large selection of new and antique quilts, quilt fabric and supplies.
✚ E5 ✉ Pike Building, 1411 1st Avenue (go inside between Pike and Union) ☎ 206/622–6382

YE OLDE CURIOSITY SHOP

Century-old store/museum with a fascinating mix of Northwest momentos – many bizarre or grotesque.
✚ G5 ✉ Pier 54 on Alaskan Way ☎ 206/682–5844

Kitsch, Funk & Retro

ARCHIE MCPHEE & CO

First stop for gag gifts and novelties including plastic cockroaches, inflatable sharks, rubber chickens and boxing nun puppets.
➕ A3 ✉ 2428 NW Market Street ☎ 206/297–0240 ▣ 17, 18 🕐 Mon–Sat 9–7; Sun 10–6

FIBBER MCGEE'S CLOSET

Vintage collectables from cookie jars to taxidermy.
➕ C5 ✉ 321 E Pine Street, Capitol Hill ☎ 206/625–2282

FREMONT ANTIQUE MALL

Different dealers carrying all-American memorabilia, vintage clothes and collectables. Armadillo lamps to an autographed Charles Manson painting.
➕ A2 ✉ 3419 Fremont Place N ☎ 206/548–9140 🕐 Mon–Sun 10–6

FRITZI RITZ

Men's and women's vintage clothing, hats, shoes and wigs labelled by decade.
➕ A2 ✉ 3425 Fremont Place N ☎ 206/633–0929 🕐 Tue–Fri 12–6; Sat noon–5:30; Sun noon–5

ISADORAS

High-end vintage finery: beaded cocktail dresses, vintage gowns and, for men, suits, hats and ties.
➕ E5 ✉ 1915 First Avenue, 2 blocks north of Market ☎ 206/441–77110

LE FROCK

Recycled and vintage clothing for both men and women.
➕ C5 ✉ 317 E Pine Street, Capitol Hill ☎ 206/623–5339

RED LIGHT

Glitzy platform shoes, wigs, retro pants and tops.
➕ Off map at A5 ✉ 4560 University Way NE
☎ 206/545–4044 ▣ 71, 72, 73, 43

RETRO VIVA

Retro apparel and jewellery at three locations.
➕ E5 ✉ 1511 1st Avenue ☎ 206/624–2529
➕ D4 ✉ 215 Broadway E ☎ 206/328–7451
➕ A6 ✉ 4515 University Way NE ☎ 206/632–8886 ▣ 71, 72, 73, 43

RHINESTONE ROSIE

Estate and costume jewellery treasures, 1870–1970, restored and repaired. For sale or hire.
➕ B2 ✉ 606 W Crockett, Queen Anne ☎ 206/283–4605 🕐 Tue–Fri 11–5; Sat 11–4

ROOTIE KAZOOTIES

Fifties collectables, cards, novelties and gifts for the young at heart.
➕ C5 ✉ 324 15th Avenue E, Capitol Hill ☎ 206/325–9178 🕐 Mon–Sat 10–6; Sun 11–5

RUDY'S VINTAGE

Primarily 1950's and 1960's men's clothes, shirts, fedoras, suits and trousers. Stacey Adams shoes.
➕ D3 ✉ 109 Pine Street (1st–2nd), Downtown ☎ 206/682–6586 🕐 Mon–Sat 10:30–6; Sun noon–5

TIME TUNNEL

Men's and women's fashion from the 1970's and earlier.
➕ E5 ✉ 1914 2nd Avenue ☎ 206/448–1030

FREMONT FUNK

With *De Libertas Quirkas* (the right to be quirky) as its motto, it's no wonder that Seattle's Fremont neighbourhood is both the birthplace and breeding ground of local funk. In the 1960s and 1970s artists, bohemians and students began moving into old brick buildings that had fallen into disrepair. Attracted by low rents, these new residents set up studios, shops and cafés that established a playful, down-home aesthetic. Before long, they'd formed the Fremont Arts Council charged with helping create a sense of community through art…and not the highbrow art of cultural institutions, but accessible art with a sense of humour. Their concept of art embraced both whimsical public sculptures like *Waiting for the Interurban*, and the *Fremont Troll* (▶ 53), and community festivals and events.

Theatre and Film

DID YOU KNOW?

• Theatre

Seattle is nationally known for its dynamic theatre scene. Professional companies offer an awesome range of material including classical, contemporary and experimental productions. Each spring the Fringe Theater Festival features dozens of shows in various locations – primarily on Capitol Hill.

• Film

In addition, Seattle is a great place for film buffs. The city hosts an annual International Film Festival in May and June that is the largest in the United States. Other festivals include Women in Cinema and Jewish, Irish and Asian festivals.

THEATRE

A CONTEMPORARY THEATER (ACT)

Contemporary plays May–December; the season always closes with *A Christmas Carol*. Downtown.
➕ C2 ✉ 700 Union Street
☎ 206/292–7676

CREPE DE PARIS

Seattle's downtown dinner theatre; French cuisine and cabaret. Terrace. Reservations recommended.
➕ F6 ✉ 1333 5th Avenue at Rainier Square
☎ 206/623–4111 🕐 Mon–Sat

THE EMPTY SPACE THEATER

Bold, imaginative theatrical presentations in funky Fremont.
➕ A3 ✉ 3509 Fremont Avenue N ☎ 206/547–7500 🚌 26

FIFTH AVENUE THEATER

This historic, ornate hall hosts new productions of classic musicals and touring Broadway shows.
➕ F6 ✉ 1308 5th Avenue
☎ 206/625–1900

INTIMAN THEATER

Pulitzer Prize-winning regional company that focuses on modern plays and the classics. Season runs May–December.
➕ C2 ✉ 201 Mercer Street, Seattle Center ☎ 206/269–1900 🚌 1, 2, 13

PARAMOUNT THEATER

A lovingly restored 1920s movie palace that stages touring Broadway blockbusters.
➕ E6 ✉ 911 Pine Street
☎ 206/682–1414

NORTHWEST ASIAN–AMERICAN THEATER

The Northwest's only Asian-American theatre mounts productions in the International District.
➕ E4 ✉ 409 7th Avenue S at Jackson ☎ 206/340–1445

SEATTLE REPERTORY THEATER

Seattle's oldest theatre company, presents updated classics, recent off-Broadway and regional plays and premiers of works by up-and-coming playwrights. Season runs October–May.
➕ C2 ✉ Bagley Wright Theater, Seattle Center ☎ 206/443–2222
🚌 1, 2, 13, 15, 18

FILM HOUSES

GUILD 45TH

Two neighbouring theatres in the Wallingford district.
➕ A6 ✉ 2115 N 45th Street
☎ 206/633–3353

THE EGYPTIAN

This former Masonic Temple features non-mainstream current releases.
➕ C5 ✉ 801 E Pine Street (Capitol Hill) ☎ 206/323–4978

HARVARD EXIT

Consistently strong programming featuring off-beat current releases in an old Capitol Hill Mansion.
➕ C4 ✉ 807 E Roy
☎ 206/323–8986

SEVEN GABLES

This cosy, converted residence in the University District features arthouse films.
➕ A6 ✉ 911 NE 50th Street
☎ 206/632–5545

Classical Music, Dance & Opera

CLASSICAL MUSIC

FRYE MUSEUM CONCERT SERIES

The Ladies Musical Club presents free Sunday afternoon chamber music concerts at 2PM roughly twice a month at the Frye.

➕ E4 ✉ 704 Terry Avenue
☎ 206/622–9250 🚌 3, 4

INTERNATIONAL CHAMBER MUSIC SERIES

Renowned chamber music ensembles perform from fall to spring at the University of Washington.

➕ A5 ✉ Meany Theater, University of Washington, 4001 University Way NE
☎ 206/543–4880

OLYMPIC MUSIC FESTIVAL

The Philadelphia String Quartet and other celebrated musicians perform in a turn-of-the-century barn on the Olympic Peninsula near Port Townsend, June–September.

➕ A5 ☎ 206/527–8839; www.musicfest.net

SEATTLE CHAMBER MUSIC FESTIVAL

Popular summer series performances, with pre-concert dining on the lawns of the picturesque Lakeside School.

➕ A4 ✉ Lakeside School, 14050 1st Avenue NE
☎ 206/283–8808 🚌 307 to Northgate, then 317

SEATTLE SYMPHONY ORCHESTRA

A wide variety of classical music concerts September through mid-June held in Benaroya Hall.

➕ C3 ✉ 2nd and University
☎ 206/215–4747

DANCE

MEANY HALL'S WORLD DANCE SERIES

This October–May series features ballet, modern and ethnic dance; Seattle native Mark Morris is a frequent presence.

➕ A5 ✉ Meany Hall, University of Washington campus
☎ 206/543–4880

ON THE BOARDS/ CENTER FOR CONTEMPORARY PERFORMANCE

Presentations integrate dance, theatre, music and visual media.

➕ C2 ✉ 100 West Roy
☎ 206/217–9888 🚌 15, 18

PACIFIC NORTHWEST BALLET

Renowned company under the direction of former New York City Ballet dancers. The repertory mixes contemporary and classical, including rarely performed Balanchine ballets.

➕ C3 ✉ Phelps Center, 301 Mercer Street, Seattle Center
☎ 206/441–9411 🚌 1, 2, 13

OPERA

SEATTLE OPERA

One of the nation's preeminent opera companies, with four or five full-scale productions September through May.

➕ C3 ✉ Opera House, 321 Mercer Street, Seattle Center
☎ 206/389–7676
🚌 1, 2, 13

TICKET/TICKET

Ticket sells remaining tickets for music, dance, theatre and comedy venues at half-price on the day of the show. Cash only, at two locations:

➕ F5 ✉ Pike Place Market at the 1st and Pike Information booth ⏰ Every day except Mon, noon–6PM

➕ D4 ✉ Broadway Market, second level, 401 Broadway E at E Harrison ⏰ Tue–Sat, 10–7; Sun noon–6

SEATTLE OUTDOOR CONCERT SERIES

In summer, Seattleites enjoy several outdoor concert series including:
• Out-to-Lunch noontime 'brown bag' concerts at various downtown locations.
• Wednesday evening folk and pop concerts at the Woodland Park zoo bandshell.
• Summer Nights at the Pier, a waterfront concert series featuring big-name performers of pop, rock, R&B and blues. Third week of June through late August.

➕ F5 ✉ Pier 62/63 by the Aquarium ☎ Hotline: 206/281–8111; www.onereel.org

Rock, Jazz & Blues Venues

JOINT COVER

A number of Pioneer Square Blues and Jazz Clubs offer a joint cover for club-hopping. They include: Bohemian Café, Central Saloon, Larry's, the Old Timers Café and The New Orleans.

ALL-AGES VENUES

• RKCNDY (pronounced 'rock candy') presents both local and international acts. All ages admitted; bring earplugs.
✉ 1812 Yale Avenue
☎ 206/667–0219
• Paradox – This converted film house in the University District offers shows for all ages.
✉ 5510 University Way NE
☎ 206/524–7677

BALTIC ROOM

This elegant, trendy lounge which opened in 1997 features live music – mostly piano jazz, stiff drinks and a Wednesday 'jungle night'. Dancing, too.
✚ E6 ✉ 1207 Pine Street
☎ 206/625–4444

THE BREAKROOM

Live music, both local and touring bands, tending towards punk at this Capitol Hill establishment. Bar, pool, some food.
✚ F6 ✉ 1325 E Madison Street ☎ 206/860–5155

CONOR-BYRNE'S PUBLIC HOUSE

This traditional Irish pub features live bands Thursday through Saturday, an Irish jam session Sundays at 9 and set dancing on a regular basis.
✚ Off map ✉ 5140 Ballard Avenue NW ☎ 206/784–3640;
www.conorspub.com

CROCODILE

Hippest local and national touring bands play here at this birthplace of grunge, still co-owned by wife of REM guitarist Peter Buck.
✚ E5 ✉ 2200 2nd Avenue
☎ 206/441–5611

DIMITRIOU'S JAZZ ALLEY

Legendary jazz performers in a pleasant setting. Dinner before ensures a good seat.
✚ D3 ✉ 2033 Sixth Avenue
☎ 206/441–9729;
www.jazzalley.com for schedule information

FENIX/FENIX UNDERGROUND

Live music every Thursday and Saturday, and alternating Wednesdays and Fridays. Rock to reggae to world music.
✚ G6 ☎ 206/467–1111;
www.fenixunderground.com

GRATEFUL BREAD CAFÉ

This soup and sandwich bakery by day turns into an acoustic folk club by night. Seattle Folklore Society maintains the schedule.
✚ Off map ✉ 7001 35th Avenue NE, N Seattle
☎ 206/525–3166 (café);
206/782–0505 (folk club schedule)

LARRY'S BLUES CLUB

Blues, R&B and burgers in Pioneer Square.
✚ G6 ✉ 209 1st Avenue S
☎ 206/624–7665

NEW ORLEANS CREOLE RESTAURANT

Cajun zydeco and jazz in Pioneer Square.
✚ G6 ✉ 114 1st Avenue S
☎ 206/622–2563

EL GAUCHO PAMPAS ROOM

Jazz supper club open Friday and Saturday nights. Round tables, understated lighting, a large dance floor and a stage big enough for large bands. Cabaret-style entertainment. Latin jazz and world music.
✚ D3 ✉ 90 Wall Street
☎ 206/728–1140

SIT 'N' SPIN

Seattle sound: do your laundry, play board games, eat black bean chilli or foccacia sandwiches and listen to up-and-coming Seattle rock groups before they hit the Crocodile.
✚ E5 ✉ 2219 4th Avenue
☎ 206/441–9484

Other Venues & Hang-outs

BELLTOWN BILLIARDS

This high-class bar, pool hall and Italian restaurant presents live jazz on Sunday and Monday and a Chardonnay 'happy hour' weekdays between 4–7PM with half-price pool.

✚ E5 ✉ 90 Blanchard ☎ 206/448–6779 🕐 Tue–Fri 11:30AM–2AM; Sat–Mon 4PM–2AM

COMEDY UNDERGROUND

National and local comedy acts with audience participation. Located under Swannie's Restaurant.

✚ G6 ✉ 222 S Main Street ☎ 206/628–0303 🕐 Daily

GAMEWORKS

Video arcade features state-of-the-art games. Especially popular with teens and twenty-somethings.

✚ F6 ✉ 1511 7th Avenue ☎ 206/521–0952 or 206/521–9293

GIGGLES

Microbrews on tap, cheap eats and hit-and-miss comedy. College crowd. Thursdays and Sundays are open mike comic showcase nights. University District.

✚ A6 ✉ 5220 Roosevelt Way NE ☎ 206/526–5653 🚌 66

GLOBE CAFE

Free open-mike poetry on Tuesdays and Sundays. Sunday spoken-word events have been produced by Red Sky Poetry for almost 20 years, making these the longest continuously running events of their kind on the West Coast.

✚ D5 ✉ 1531 14th Avenue ☎ 206/633–5647

JILLIAN'S BILLIARD CLUB & CAFE

Two floors of pool and a restaurant plus the original bar from New York's Algonquin Hotel.

✚ D3 ✉ 731 Westlake N ☎ 206/223–0300 🕐 Weekdays till 2AM, weekends till 4AM

911 MEDIA ARTS

Experimental film and video; cutting-edge workshops and classes.

✚ D3 ✉ 117 Yale Avenue N (near REI) ☎ 206/682–6552

PACIFIC SCIENCE CENTER LASER SHOWS

Laser light shows to rock music Tuesday to Sunday evenings.

✚ D2 ✉ 2nd N at Seattle Center ☎ 206/443–2850 🚌 1, 2,13, 15, 18, 24, 33

RICHARD HUGO HOUSE

Seattle's welcoming literary arts gathering place. Frequent readings and other programming.

✚ D4 ✉ 1634 11th Avenue ☎ 206/322–7030

THEATERSPORTS

Unexpected Productions presents improvisational drama evenings at the Market Theater.

✚ F5 ✉ 1428 Post Alley at the Pike Street Market ☎ 206/781–9273

UNIVERSITY OF WASHINGTON OBSERVATORY

During inclement weather, see a slide show on astronomy. Free star-gazing Monday to Thursday 9–11PM.

✚ A6 ✉ Entrance to campus at NE 45th and 17th Avenue NE ☎ 206/543–0126

SEATTLE AND THE SPOKEN WORD

Each year Seattle hosts a vast number and variety of literary events, from the distinguished Seattle Arts and Literature series running September through May in which some of the world's finest writers speak and read from their work. Other spoken word venues include Seattle's annual Poetry Festival held the last weekend in April through the first weekend in May, and the weekly poetry slams each Wednesday night at the Sit 'n' Spin (➤ 80). As a member of National Poetry Slam Inc., slam producers abide by the four basic poetry slam rules: 1. No props; 2. Must be original material performed by the author; 3. Don't go over 3 minutes; 4. 'Check your ego at the door'. Judges are chosen from the audience.

☎ 206/725–1650 for information on Seattle poetry slams; www.seattleartsand lectures.org; www.poetryfestival.org

Bars, Pubs & Taverns

GAY SEATTLE

Seattle's liberal attitudes and acceptance of alternative lifestyles has attracted a sizeable gay and lesbian population centred around Capitol Hill's Pike/Pine corridor. Tracing its roots to the 1930s, the population increased after 1946 when gay servicemen stationed nearby moved to the city. In 1969, Dorian House was established 'to provide counselling and employment help to homosexuals in the Seattle area'. It was the first organisation of its kind in the United States. Some five years later, Seattle held a Gay Pride celebration featuring a parade down Broadway followed by a rally at Volunteer Park. While the first march attracted only about 2,000 participants and a raft of protesters, a recent rally drew an estimated 75,000 people, both gay and straight, to walk together in solidarity. Seattle's established gay and lesbian bars include: Neighbours ✉ 1509 Broadway ☎ 206/324–5358; Timberline ✉ 2015 Boren Avenue ☎ 206/883–0242; and Wildrose ✉ 1021 E Pike ☎ 206/324–9210. The *Seattle Gay News* is a good local source of information.

FIRESIDE ROOM

With its over-stuffed chairs and fireplace, this spot in the lobby of the stately Sorrento Hotel takes you back to earlier, more genteel times.
✚ F6 ✉ 900 Madison Street ☎ 206/622–6400

FX MCRORY'S STEAK CHOP & OYSTER HOUSE

With a first-rate oyster bar, more than 140 bourbons and 26 beers on tap, this sparkling brass-and-wood establishment across from the Kingdome attracts both professional athletes and sports fans. Full bar; noisy.
✚ G6 ✉ 419 Occidental Avenue S ☎ 206/623–4800 🕐 Till midnight

HARBOUR PUBLIC HOUSE

Wonderful neighbourhood pub just a short walk from the ferry dock, on Bainbridge Island. Good burgers, fish'n'chips and pasta.
✚ L2 ✉ 231 Parfitt Way SW on Bainbridge ☎ 206/842–0969

HOPSCOTCH

With 60 single-malt Scotches, 16 microbrews and good food in a pleasant Capitol Hill setting.
✚ D5 ✉ 332 15th Avenue E ☎ 206/322–4191 🕐 10

KELL'S IRISH RESTAURANT & PUB

The elegance of a Dublin supper room and the warmth of an Irish pub. Irish music. A market favourite.
✚ F5 ✉ 1916 Post Alley ☎ 206/728–1916

THE PIKE PUB & BREWERY

Frequented by Seattleites for its good food and excellent craft beers. The microbrew museum is also worth a look.
✚ F5 ✉ 1415 First Avenue (in the Market) ☎ 622–6044 🕐 Till midnight

QUEEN CITY GRILL

Belltown's classiest pub. The first-rate kitchen specialises in grilled entrées. Chic, crowded and noisy.
✚ E5 ✉ 2201 1st Avenue ☎ 206/443–0975

VIRGINIA INN

A Seattle institution – with art on the walls and a posted quotation providing food for thought for an eclectic group of patrons.
✚ E5 ✉ 1937 1st Avenue ☎ 206/728–1937 🕐 Mon–Thu 11AM– midnight; Fri–Sat 11AM–2AM; Sun noon–midnight

VON'S GRAND CITY CAFÉ

The city's best martini 'or your money back'. Prime rib and fruitwood-smoked turkey stand out in this classic dark wood establishment papered with political cartoons from Seattle papers, quirky memorabilia, photographs and witty quotes.
✚ E6 ✉ 619 Pine St ☎ 206/621–8667

Spectator Sports Venues

BASEBALL

The Seattle Mariners play at Safeco Field, the 'state-of-the-art' ballpark that opened in 1999. The open-air stadium seats 47,000 and has a retractable roof that can be closed in bad weather. Baseball season runs from spring into autumn; Safeco tours are available year round.

✚ F3 ✉ 1250 1st Avenue S at Royal Brougham ☎ 206/346–4287 for tickets; www.seattlemariners.com

BASKETBALL

The Seattle SuperSonics, the city's oldest professional sports franchise, play at home in Key Arena October to April.

✚ D2 ✉ 1st Avenue N ☎ 206/628–0888 (Ticketmaster); www.nba.com/sonics 🚌 1, 2, 13

The Seattle Storm is the city's newest professional sports team. A member of the WNBA, this women's team plays in Key Arena from the end of May through the middle of August.

✚ D2 ✉ 1st Avenue N at Seattle Center ☎ 206/628–0888 (Tickemaster)

FOOTBALL

Seattle's NFL team, the Seahawks, play September through December. Until 2002 they will play at Husky Stadium at the University of Washington (see panel). Most games are on Sundays at 1PM.

✚ A5 ☎ 1–888/NFL-HAWK; www.seahawks.com 🚌 71, 72, 73, 43, 25

The University of Washington's Huskies play PAC-10 football in autumn at the Husky Stadium. Games are on Saturday.

✚ A5 ✉ Montlake Boulevard NE ☎ 206/543–2200

HOCKEY

The WHL's Seattle Thunderbirds play in Key Arena September to May.

✚ D2 ✉ 400 1st Avenue N ☎ 206/728–9121; www.seattle-thunderbirds.com 🚌 1, 2, 13, 15, 18

HORSE-RACING

Emerald Downs, Auburn. Thoroughbred racing from March through September. Special events in summer.

✚ N3 ✉ 2300 Emerald Downs Drive, Auburn ☎ 206/288–7000, Toll-free 1–888/931–8400; www.emeralddowns.com 🕐 First race weekdays at 5, weekends and holidays at 1

HYDROPLANE RACES

Held every August since 1950 on a 2-mile course south of the Lake Washington floating bridge.

✚ L3 ☎ 206/728–0123 for viewing area tickets

SOCCER

The Seattle Sounders, the city's professional men's soccer team, play at the Memorial Stadium. Season runs April to October.

✚ B3 ✉ 5th Avenue N ☎ 1–800/796–KICK; www.seattlesounders.com 🚌 1, 2, 15, 18

TICKETMASTER

Tickets to many of Seattle's sporting events, as well as concerts, are available from this outlet.

☎ 206/628–0888

DID YOU KNOW?

After speculation that the Seattle Seahawks football team would leave Seattle, billionaire Paul Allen, co-founder of Microsoft, stepped to the plate in 1997 and bought the team. The following summer, Seattle voters approved a referendum to tear down the massive Kingdome and build a new open-air football stadium on its site. The new facility, which will include an exhibition centre, is scheduled to open in the summer of 2002. The new stadium will also accommodate Seattle Sounder soccer games.

Luxury Hotels

**Expect to pay the following
per night for a double room:**

£ = under $85
££ = $85–150
£££ = Over $150

DISCOUNTS AND
PROMOTIONS

Many of the larger hotels
and some smaller ones offer
special corporate rates
or discounts. Some
establishments accept
Entertainment cards, which
can reduce prices by 50 per
cent; those catering to
business travellers may have
reduced rates at weekends; in
addition, most establishments
lower their rates in the off-
season.

ALEXIS HOTEL (£££)
Small downtown hotel
with tasteful postmodern
styling and impeccable
service, 109 guest rooms.
Renovated in 1996.
✚ F6 ✉ 1007 1st Avenue
☎ 206/624–4844 or
800/426–7033

FOUR SEASONS
OLYMPIC HOTEL (£££)
Built in 1924 and remodelled in 1982, many consider
this Seattle's best hotel.
Spa and pool plus the
lavish Georgian Room. With
450 rooms, fitness centre,
bar, lounge, restaurants
and shops on-site.
✚ F6 ✉ 411 University Street
☎ 206/621–1700

HOTEL MONACO (£££)
Built in 1997, 189 rooms.
Lively and stylish;
personable staff and fun
restaurant – Sazerac. Some
rooms have two-person
soaking baths.
✚ F6 ✉ 1101 4th Avenue
☎ 206/621–1770;
fax: 206/624–0060

INN AT HARBOR STEPS
(£££)
Elegant retreat near
Seattle Art Museum and
waterfront. The 20 rooms
are well-appointed. Fit-
ness centre, pool and spa.
✚ F6 ✉ 1221 1st Avenue
☎ Toll-free 888-728–8910

INN AT THE MARKET
(£££)
This charming 69-room
hotel with French provin-
cial decor shares a brick
courtyard with Campagne
Restaurant. Courtesy car.
✚ F5 ✉ 86 Pine Street
☎ 206/443–3600 or 800-
446–4484; fax: 206/448–0631

MAYFLOWER PARK
(£££)
An elegant hotel with
172 rooms in a renovated
1920s building near
Westlake Center. Small
workout facility. Home
of the popular bar/lounge
and the romantic
Andaluca Restaurant.
✚ E5 ✉ 405 Olive Way
☎ 206/ 623–8700; fax:
206/382–6996

RESIDENCE INN BY
MARRIOTT-LAKE
UNION (££–£££)
The 234 well-appointed
rooms have fully-equipped
kitchens and living rooms.
Complimentary
continental breakfasts,
fitness centre, pool and
courtesy car. Pets allowed.
✚ C4 ✉ 800 Fairview Avenue
N ☎ 206/624–6000 or
1–800/331–3131;
www.residenceinn.com/seattle

SHERATON SEATTLE
HOTEL & TOWERS (£££)
Downtown tower with a
striking lobby and 840
luxury rooms filled with art
by Northwest artists.
Health club and Fullers
Restaurant; first-rate
concierge staff. Childcare.
✚ E6 ✉ 1400 6th Avenue
☎ 206/621–9000;
www.sheraton.com/seattle

WESTIN SEATTLE (£££)
Large downtown hotel
with an attractive lobby
and a fine concierge and
bell staff, 865 rooms.
Fitness centre and
Nikko's Restaurant. In-
room modem hook-ups.
Small pets allowed.
✚ E5 ✉ 1900 5th Avenue at
Stewart ☎ 800/228–3000;
fax: 206/728–2259

Mid-Range Hotels

BEST WESTERN EXECUTIVE INN (££)
123 new units near the Seattle Center. Restaurant/ lounge. Free parking.
➕ D3 ✉ 200 Taylor N
☎ 206/448–9444;
www.bwexec-inn.com 🚌 3, 4, 16

BEST WESTERN PIONEER SQUARE HOTEL (££–£££)
Restored hotel in Pioneer Square, with 75 rooms. Corporate discounts available.
➕ G6 ✉ 77 Yesler Way
☎ 206/340-1234,
fax: 206/467–0707;
www.pioneersquare.com

EXECUTIVE EXTENDE D STAY (££)
Furnished apartment suites near hospitals on south Capitol Hill. Units have kitchens, washer-dryer, telephones with private lines and data ports; fitness centre, spa. Complimentary shuttle.
➕ D4 ✉ 300 10th Avenue
☎ 206/223–9300,
1–800/906–6226;
fax: 206/233–0241

EXECUTIVE PACIFIC PLAZA HOTEL (££)
Convenient downtown location with 160 rooms; continental breakfast; Red Robin bar and restaurant.
➕ F6 ✉ 400 Spring Street
☎ 206/623–3900 or
800/426–1165, fax: 623–2059

HAMPTON INN DOWNTOWN (££)
This new motor inn at Seattle Center has an attractive lobby and 124 comfortable rooms. Continental breakfast,

premium cable TV, 24-hour fitness room. Free parking. Excellent value.
➕ D3 ✉ 700 5th Avenue North ☎ 206/282–7700 or 800/HAMPTON; fax: 206/282–0899; www.hamptoninn.com 🚌 3, 4 , 16; Monorail to downtown.

HAWTHORN INN AND SUITES (££)
Between downtown and Seattle Center, this hotel has 72 rooms. Free local calls and free parking. Complimentary breakfast, sauna and spa, fitness room and free bike hire.
➕ D3 ✉ 2224 8th Avenue
☎ 206/624–6820 or
1–800/437–4867

HOTEL SEATTLE (££)
Downtown hotel with 81 rooms; renovated in 1996. Restaurant/lounge serves breakfast and lunch.
➕ F6 ✉ 315 Seneca
☎ 206/623–5110 and
800/426–2439; fax: 206/623–5110

SILVER CLOUD INN (££)
This inn has 180 units with mini kitchens. Swimming pool, fitness centre, complimentary continental breakfast; free local calls. University Village area.
➕ A6 ✉ 5036 25th Avenue NE ☎ 206/526–5200,
1–800/205–6940;
www.scinns.com

WESTCOAST VANCE HOTEL (££)
Lovingly restored hotel. The 165 rooms and baths are tiny but immaculate. Bar and restaurant on-site.
➕ E6 ✉ 620 Stewart Street
☎ 206/441–4200,
1–800/325–4000;
fax: 306/441–8612;
www.westcoasthotels.com/vance

ONLINE LODGING GUIDES AND SERVICES

• www.seeseattle.org
Seattle/King County Convention and Visitor's Bureau website contains a lodging guide and online coupons which can be printed and used for discounted rates.

• A Pacific Reservation Service has a website at www.seattlebedandbreakfast.com. Click on 'What I really want is a place…' and then on 'Inexpensive Rates' for several appealing lodging options in residential areas.

• www.Seattlehotelguide.net

• www.seattletravel.com

Budget Accommodation

HOTELS

COLLEGE INN GUEST HOUSE (££)
The upper floors of this 1904 Tudor building house a pension with 25 rooms, each with a bed, wash basin, writing desk and chair, and shared bathroom. Bountiful continental breakfast. Café and pub downstairs.
✚ A5 ✉ 4000 University Way NE ☎ 206/633–4441

KINGS INN (££)
Friendly staff, 68 rooms and a great downtown location across from the monorail. Cable TV, laundry. Free parking. AARP, corporate and government discounts.
✚ E5 ✉ 2106 5th Avenue ☎ 800/546–4760; fax: 206/441–0730

TUGBOAT CHALLENGER BUNK & BREAKFAST (£–££)
Renovated tugboat moored on Lake Union with eight nautical-motif cabins. Five cabins have private baths and tub or shower. TV/VCR's in rooms. Salon with fireplace on premises.
✚ C4 ✉ 1001 Fairview Avenue N ☎ 206/340–1201; fax: 206/621–9208

UNIVERSITY MOTEL (£)
Large suites on a quiet street in the University district. Twenty-one units with separate bedrooms, kitchens, pullout bed in living room and cable TV. Plain, dated furnishings, but plenty of room to swing a cat. Laundry; free parking. Per person charge.

✚ A6 ✉ 4731 12th Avenue NE ☎ 206/522–4724; toll-free at 1–800/522–1720

HOSTELS

GREEN TORTOISE HOSTEL (£)
At the Pike Place Market. Thirty-seven rooms, shared and private: linen provided. Shared kitchen and common room with stereo, TV and VCR; lockers and laundry facilities. Free internet service, free breakfast, area discount card, 24-hour check-in.
✚ F5 ✉ 1525 2nd Avenue ☎ 206/340–1222 or 1–888/424–6783; www.greentortoise.net; fax: 206/623–3207; ☒ Free bus zone

HOSTELLING INTERNATIONAL SEATTLE (£)
Bunkrooms for 4–6 people for a total of 139 beds; handicapped accessible; ample shared kitchen and common room; library with travel books and other resources. Non-members welcome but AYH members are given priority in busy seasons.
✚ F5 ✉ 84 Union Street (1st-Western) ☎ 206/622–5443 or 1–888/622–5443; www.hiseattle.org

YWCA (£)
Good central downtown location. Twenty rooms with refrigerators, singles and doubles, some with private baths. Health club and swimming pool on premises.
✚ F6 ✉ 1118 5th Avenue ☎ 206/461–4888; fax 206/461–4860

BED AND BREAKFAST

GASLIGHT INN (£–££)
Lovingly restored turn-of-the-century mansion and annex. Well-appointed rooms, charming court-yard with plantings and a small swimming pool.
✚ D5 ✉ 1727 15th Avenue ☎ 206/325–3654 ☒ 10, 43

INN AT QUEEN ANNE (£–££)
Comfortable 67-room inn in an older brick building next to Seattle Center. Complimentary breakfast, kitchenettes, cable TV, voicemail and air conditioning.
✚ C2 ✉ 505 1st Avenue N ☎ 206/282–7357 or 800/952–5043 ☒ 1, 2, 13, 15, 18

SALISBURY HOUSE (£–££)
Charming, beautifully restored and decorated 1904 home on a residential street on north Capitol Hill. A gem.
✚ C5 ✉ 750 16th Avenue E ☎ 206/328–8682; fax: 206/720–1019 ☒ 10

SEATTLE
travel facts

Arriving & Departing *88–89*

Essential Facts *89–91*

Public Transport *91–92*

Media & Communications *92–93*

Emergencies *93*

ARRIVING & DEPARTING

Before you go

- A visa is required if:
  1) you are not a citizen of the Visa Waiver Programme countries (these include Australia, Ireland, New Zealand and the UK);
  2) you are staying more than 90 days;
  3) Your trip is not a holiday or short business trip;
  4) you have ever been refused a visa or admission to the US, or have been required to leave the US by the US Immigration and Naturalisation Service; or
  5) you do not have a return or onward ticket.
  Otherwise a Visa Waiver form is supplied by the airline.
- If you intend to hire a car and are not a US citizen, plan to bring your foreign licence and an international driver's licence which must be acquired before arriving. Most car hire agencies require a major credit card; many will not hire to persons under 25.

When to go

- July and August are prime months to visit – sunny and clear with usually no more than an inch of rain. Days are long with temperatures up to 85°F; nights can be quite cool. Come prepared to dress in layers.
- November to January are the rainiest months.
- Spring comes early in Seattle, bringing a flurry of bulbs and flowering trees. Despite the weather, which can be unsettled, it is a favourite time for many.
- September is often lovely, with temperatures ranging between 70°–50°F and rainfall averaging 1.88 inches.

Climate

- Moderate temperatures year-round averaging: Dec–Jan: 46°F; Mar–May: 58°F; Jun–Aug: 73°F; Sep–Nov: 53°F.
- Total annual precipitation averages 34–37 inches (less than New York and Boston). Many days are cloudy.
- Thunderstorms are rare. Snow is infrequent in Seattle, itself, but the Cascades and Olympic Mountains receive vast quantities; ski areas generally open by late November.

Arriving by air

- Sea-Tac International Airport is 13 miles south of Seattle via I-5
- An airport information desk near baggage claim provides current information on ground transport.
  Airport information:
  ☎ 206/433–5388
- Bus service to downtown hotels at half-hour intervals, 5AM–11PM via Gray Line Airport Express
  ☎ (206/626–6088
- Door-to-door van service to and from airport: Shuttle Express
  ☎ 206/622–1424 or 1–800/487–RIDE
- Taxis line up at a stand outside of baggage claim. Fares run about $25–30 without tip.
- City buses to downtown leave from Sea-Tac baggage claim level. Call Metro ☎ 206/553–3000 for schedule information.

Arriving by bus

- Greyhound Bus Lines
  ✉ 811 Stewart Street connects Seattle to other cities.
  Greyhound Information
  ☎ 800/231–2222
- Green Tortoise Alternative Travel makes twice weekly runs between Seattle and Los Angeles.
  Call ☎ 800/867–8647

Arriving by car

- Visitors arriving by car will enter the city via I-5. Downtown exits are: Union Street (for City Center) and James Street (for Pioneer Square).
- Those arriving via I-90 from the east will cross the Lake Washington floating bridge and follow signs to I-5 north for downtown exits.

Arriving by train

- Trains arrive at King Street Station at 3rd and Jackson between Pioneer Square and the International District. Call Amtrak: ☎ 1–800/872–7245

Customs regulations

- Duty-free allowances include 1 litre of alcoholic spirits or wine (no one under 21 may bring in alcohol), 200 cigarettes or 50 cigars (not Cuban) and up tp $100-worth of gifts.
- Some medications may be prescription-only in the US and may be confiscated. Bring a doctor's certificate for essential medication.

ESSENTIAL FACTS

Electricity

- 110 volts, 60 cycles AC current.
- Electrical outlets are for flat, two-prong plugs. European appliances require an adaptor.

Etiquette

- Seattle dress is informal; for most places, a jacket and tie are optional.
- Seattle has a successful recycling programme. Many public places provide recycling bins. Littering is not tolerated.
- Most public places prohibit smoking.

- Tipping 15–20 per cent is customary in restaurants; 15 per cent for taxis.

Operating hours

- Banks: Generally Mon–Fri 9:30–5, some open Sat mornings.
- Offices: Normally Mon–Fri 9–5.
- Stores downtown open between 9–10AM and typically close at 5–6PM with some staying open till 9 on Thursday evenings. Shops in shopping malls generally stay open Mon–Sat till 9PM; Sun till 5 or 6PM.

National Holidays

New Year's Day (1 Jan); Martin Luther King Day (third Mon in Jan); President's Day (third Mon in Feb); Memorial Day (last Mon in May); Independence Day (4 July); Labor Day (first Mon in Sept); Columbus Day (second Mon in Oct); Veterans' Day (11 Nov); Thanksgiving (fourth Thu in Nov); Christmas Day (25 Dec)

Money matters

- Unit of currency is the US dollar (= 100 cents). Notes are $1, $5, $10, $20, $50 and $100; coins are 50¢ (a half-dollar), 25¢ (a quarter), 10¢ (a dime), 5¢ (a nickel) and 1¢ (a penny).
- Money-changing facilities are available at Sea-Tac Airport, banks and at Thomas Cook ✉ 9906 3rd Avenue, downtown ☎ 206/623–6203
- Most major establishments and businesses accept major credit cards. Few places accept personal cheques; bring travellers' cheques.
- Automatic Teller Machines (ATMs) are available at most banks.

Discounts

- Ticket/Ticket: Half-price day-of-show tickets (cash only): theatre, concert, dance, comedy and music

available at two locations: Pike
Place Market Info Booth ✉ 1st and
Pike and Broadway Market, 401 Broadway E on
Capitol Hill ☎ 206/324–2744 ④ Closed Mon

- A CityPass ticket book will
reduce admission prices by 50 per
cent to Woodland Park Zoo,
Seattle Art Musum, Space
Needle, Pacific Science Center,
Seattle Aquarium and Museum of
Flight. Passbooks can be
purchased at any of the six attractions and are valid for seven days.
- Student travellers are advised to
bring a current student ID to
obtain discounted admissions.

Places of worship

Check the Yellow Pages of the phone
book for complete listings. Prominent
houses of worship include:

- Catholic: St James Cathedral
✉ 9th and Marion ☎ 206/622–3559
- Congregational: Plymouth
Congregational Church ✉ 6th and
University ☎ 206/622–4865
- Episcopal: St Marks Episcopal
Cathedral ✉ 1245 10th Avenue E (Capitol
Hill) ☎ 206/323–0300
- Greek Orthodox: St Demetrios
Greek Orthodox Church
✉ 2100 Boyer E ☎ 206/325–4347
- Lutheran: Gethsemane Lutheran
Church
✉ 9th & Stewart ☎ 206/682–3620
- Methodist: First United
Methodist ✉ 811 5th Avenue
☎ 206/622–7278
- Mosque: Islamic (Idriss) Mosque
✉ 1420 NE Northgate Way ☎ 206/363–3013
- Synagogues: Temple
De Hirsch Sinai
✉ 1511 E Pike Street ☎ 206/323–8486

Public toilets

- Public toilets are located in Pike
Place Market (base of the ramp in
the Main Arcade) and in the
Convention Center.

Time differences

- Seattle is on Pacific Standard
Time, three hours behind Eastern
Standard Time in New York,
eight hours behind the UK.

Weights and measures

- Metric equivalents for US weights
and measures are:
- Weights:
1 ounce (oz) = 28 grams; 1 pound
(lb) = 0.45 kilogram;
1 quart (qt) = 0.9 litre.
- Meaurements:
1 inch (") = 2.5 centimetres;
1 foot (') =0.3 metre;
1 yard (yd) = 0.9 metre;
1 mile = 1.6 kilometres.

Visitor information

- Seattle-King County Convention
and Visitors Bureau
✉ level 1, Galleria/800 Convention Place
in the Convention Center (8th and Pike)
☎ 206/461–5840;
www.seeseattle.org ④ Mon–Fri 8:30–5,
Sat–Sun 10–4
- Seattle Center Info
☎ 206/684–7200; for recorded
events information
☎ 206/684–8582
- Seattle Public Library offers a
Quick Information number
☎ 206/386–INFO. Beginning in
June 2001, the downtown
branch of Seattle Public
Library will move to a
temporary home at 8th Avenue
and Pike, across from the
Washington State Convention
Center
④ Mon–Thu 9–9; Fri–Sat 10:3–06;
Sun 1–5
- Travellers with disabilities: there
is a 24 hour telephone operator
service for TTY
(Telecommunications Device for
the Deaf) available by dialling
☎ 1–800/855–1155

Websites for research on the Internet

- Art access including artists profiles, exhibit reviews and local venues: www.artaccess.com
- City of Seattle's comprehensive visitor information site: www.ci.seattle.wa.us
- Riderlink guide to area transport: www.riderlink.gen.wa.us
- Entertainment listings: www.seattlesidewalk.com
- Local jazz, literary happenings: www.speakeasy.org
- Events calendar from Seattle's alternative weekly: www.thestranger.com

Consulates

- Austria ✉ 111 3rd Avenue, Suite 2626 ☎ 206/633–3606
- British ✉ 900 4th Avenue, Suite 3001 ☎ 206/622–9255
- Canadian ✉ 412 Plaza 600, 6th Avenue & Stewart Street ☎ 206/443–1777
- French ✉ 801 2nd Avenue, suite 1500 ☎ 206/624–7855
- Japanese ✉ 601 Union Street, suite 500 ☎ 206/682–9107
- Mexican ✉ 2132 3rd Avenue ☎ 206/448–3526
- New Zealand ☎ 360/766–8002
- Norway ✉ 1402 3rd Avenue, Suite 806 ☎ 206/623–3957
- Russia ✉ 2001 6th Avenue, Suite 2323 ☎ 206/728–1910 🕒 Mon–Fri 9–noon
- South Korea ✉ 2033 6th Avenue, Suite 1125 ☎ 206/441–1011
- Sweden ✉ 1215 4th Avenue, Suite 1019 ☎ 206/622–5640
- Taiwan ✉ 2001 6th Avenue, Suite 2410 ☎ 206/441–4586

PUBLIC TRANSPORT

Bicycle

- The city has a number of bicycle routes or trails. For Bicycle Hire, see Active Pursuits (➤ 56–57)

Metro Buses

- For Metro Rider Information telephone ☎ 206/553–3000 or 800/542–7876; also online information www.transit.metrokc
- Timetables available at Westlake Station, on buses and at more than 500 locations around the city.
- Metro has a Ride Free Area downtown bordered by Battery Street, Jackson Street, Alaskan Way, 6th Avenue and I-5. Hours are 6AM–7PM.
- The Metro tunnels under Pine Street and 3rd Avenue with five downtown stations: Convention Place, Westlake, University Street, Pioneer Square and the International District. All tunnel routes stop at each station. Sundays and evenings after hours when the tunnel is closed, tunnel buses run above ground along 3rd Avenue.
- Seattle bus drivers are not required to call out the stops along the route. Ask your driver to alert you once you have reached your stop.

Monorail

- The 1.2-mile ride between downtown Westlake Center ✉ 400 Pine Street and Seattle Center takes only 90 seconds. Trains run every 15 minutes, 9AM–11PM.

Taxis

- Seattle taxis are expensive: the flag-drop charge is $1.80 and it's $1.80 for each additional mile. Pick one up in front of your hotel or phone for a radio-dispatched cab.
- Major companies with 24-hour

91

dispatch service include
Yellow Cab, which has merged
with Graytop Cab ☎ 206/622–6500
or 206/282–8222
Also FarWest ☎ 206/622–1717.
To summon the cab closest to
your location ☎ 1–800/USA–TAXI

Washington State ferries

- Jumbo ferries from Seattle's
downtown terminal to Bainbridge
Island and Bremerton (on the
Kitsap Peninsula) depart regularly
from Colman Dock at pier 52 and
accommodate both walk-on
passengers and cars.
- Most ferry routes are very busy
during weekday commute periods
and on sunny weekends. Expect
waits of two hours or more in summer and on holiday weekends.
- Schedules change seasonally;
☎ 206/464–6400 for schedule and
route information.
- Additional ferry routes departing
from the Seattle environs serve
the Kitsap Peninsula, Vashon
Island, Whidbey Island, Port
Townsend (Olympic Peninsula),
the San Juan Islands; and Victoria,
British Columbia.
- Credit cards not accepted.
- Passengers to Canada need pass-
ports or other proof of citizenship.

Waterfront streetcar

- A vintage 1927 trolley runs along
the waterfront on Alaskan Way
from pier 70 at Broad Street to 5th
and Jackson in the International
District with intermediate stops at
Vine, Bell, Pike, University, Madison,
Washington Streets and at
Occidental Park in Pioneer Square.
- When you board, pay your fare
and ask for a transfer, which is
good for 90 minutes of sightseeing
before reboarding. Total ride, end
to end, takes 20 minutes. Service

every 20 minutes to half an hour,
Mon–Fri 7–6; Sat–Sun 9:30–6
with extended summer hours.

Community transit buses

- Bus service to points outside the
city ☎ 1–800/562–1375

MEDIA & COMMUNICATIONS

Cybercafes and e-mail access

- Seattle has a number of places
where internet access is available.
- Some hotels have DSL
connections for travellers with
laptops whilst others offer online
computer use. Branches of the
Seattle Public Library have
workstations for hire to the public.
- Capitol Hill Net ✉ 219 Broadway
☎ 206/860–6858
- Online Coffee Company (23 locations) advertise 20 minutes for
free with the purchase of coffee or
tea, and 1 free hour before 9AM
✉ Online (downtown) 111 1st Avenue (Spring-
Seneca) ☎ 206/381–1911 🕒 Tue–Thu
7AM–10PM; Fri 7AM–11PM; Sat 9AM–7PM; Sun 9AM–8PM
✉ Online (Capitol Hill) 1720 E Olive Way
☎ 206/328–3731

Mail

- Post offices: The main downtown
post office is on the corner of
Union and 3rd Avenue. Hours are
Mon–Fri 8–5:30. Closed Sat–Sun.
Branch offices are located in
most neighbourhoods. Call
☎ 1–800/275–8777 for 24-hour
infoline with Zip codes, postal
rates, post office hours and location; or www.usps.com.
- Stamps can be bought at many
supermarket check-out counters.

Telephones

- To make a local call from a pay
phone, listen for a dial tone, then

deposit coins; wait for new dial tone and dial the number.

- Phonecards for long-distance calls are available at most shops.
- To pay cash for long-distance calls, follow the same initial procedure as for local calls, and a recorded operator message will tell you how much additional money to deposit for the first three minutes; then deposit additional coins and dial.
- The area running east of Lake Washington from Everett to Maple Valley and east to Snoqualmie pass uses area code (425). The (253) area code runs south from Renton to the Pierce-Thurston county line. Other calls within western Washington require dialing a (360) area code.
- Directory assistance is a toll call. For information, dial 1 plus the area code plus the number plus the 555–1212.

Newspapers and magazines

- Seattle has two daily papers: *The Seattle Times* ☎ 206/464–2111 and the *Seattle Post-Intelligencer* ☎ 206/44–8000.
- Weeklies with extensive entertainment listings include the alternative *Stranger* and *The Weekly*. Both are free.
- *The Seattle Gay News* – a community newspaper ☎ 206/324–4297.
- International newspapers are sold at *First and Pike News* ✉ 93 Pike Street at the Pike Place Market and at *Bulldog News* ✉ 401 Broadway E

Radio and Television:

- Seattle's two National Public Radio stations (NPR) are KUOW at 94.9 FM (all-talk radio with news from the BBC) and KPLU, an award-winning jazz station at 88.5 FM.
- KING-FM (98.1) Classical music.

- Seattle's six local television channels are: KOMO 4 (ABC); KING 5 (NBC); 7 (CBS); KCTS/9 (PBS); KSTW 11 (independent); and 13 (Fox).

EMERGENCIES

Emergency phone numbers

- Police, ambulance or fire: ☎ 911
- The Red Cross Language Bank provides free, on-call interpretive assistance in emergency or crisis situations. Volunteers in over 60 languages. ☎ 206/323–2345

Safety/crime

- Exercise caution and at night avoid the areas around 1st to 2nd and Pike, the edges of Pioneer Square, and the area between 2nd and 4th from Cherry to Yesler.
- Seattle police are well-known for ticketing jaywalkers.

Lost property

- Airport lost and found ☎ 206/433–5312
- King Street Station lost and found ☎ 206/382–4128; Metro bus lost and found ☎ 206/553–3090

Medical treatment

- US Healthworks operates several drop-in clinics; nearest clinic to downtown is the clinic at Denny and Fairview ☎ 206/682-7418 🕐 Mon–Fri 7AM–6PM, Sat 9–3. Also at ✉ 8313 Aurora Avenue N ☎ 206/784–0737 🕐 Mon–Fri 8AM–7PM, Sat 9AM–5PM
- Doctor's, Inc. ☎ 206/622-9933 can help find a doctor 24 hours a day.
- Dentist Referral Service ☎ 206/443-7607
- **24-hour pharmacies**
  Bartell Drug Store ✉ 600 1st Avenue N (near Seattle Center ☎ 206/284–1354)
- Walgreen Drug Store ✉ 5409 15th Avenue NW ☎ 206/781–0056

Index

A

accommodation 84–86
aerial tours 19
airport and air services 88–89
Alki Beach 25
Allen, Paul 31
architecture 54
art and antiques shops 73
art, public 53
Automatic Teller Machines (ATMs) 89

B

bagels 69
Bainbridge Island 34
Bainbridge Island Winery 59
Ballard Locks 26
banks 89
bars, pubs and taverns 82
baseball 83
basketball 83
beaches 50–51
bed and breakfast 85
Belltown 55
bike hire 56–57
bike trails 56
Blake Island 19
Bloedel Reserve 34
boat rentals 57
Boeing Tour 48
bookshops 74
brewery tours 59
Burke-Gilman Trail 56, 57
Burke Museum 46
buses 88, 91
Butchart Gardens 20

C

Capitol Hill 55
Carl S English Botanical Gardens 26
Cascade Mountains 6
CD and tape shops 74
Chapel of St Ignatius 54
children's attractions 60
Children's Museum 60
Chinook 12
Citypass 89
classical music 59, 79
climate 6, 8, 9, 88
clothing shops 70–72
comedy venues 83
Common Meals Café 63
consulates 91
Coupeville 21
credit cards 89

crime and personal safety 93
cultural life 7
currency 89

D

dance 79
Dancers' Series: Steps 53
Daybreak Star Art Center 24
Deception Pass 21
dental treatment 93
discounted rates/admissions 89
Discovery Park 24
Downtown Seattle 14, 38
driving to Seattle 89
Dungeness Spit 21

E

eating out 62–69
economy 6–7
electricity 88–89
Elliott Bay 9
Elliott Bay Book Company readings 39, 59
Elliott Bay Park 18
emergencies 93
emergency phone numbers 93
entertainment 78–83
etiquette 89
events and festivals 22
excursions 20–21
Experience Music Project 31

F

Farmers' Market 59
ferries 34, 92
Fifth Avenue Theater 54, 78
Fishermen's Terminal 27
Fishermen's Memorial 27
fishing 57
football 83
Fort Casey 21
free events 59
free and nearly free attractions 58
Freeway Park 50
Fremont 55, 75
Fremont Troll 53
Frye Art Museum 52
Frye Museum concerts 59
Fun Forest Amusement Park 60

G

Gasworks Park 50
Gates, Bill 8
Gehry, Frank 31
gifts and souvenirs 75
Glacier Peak 6
glass-blowing demonstrations 58
Golden Gardens Beach Park 50
golf 57
Green Lake 18

H

Harbor Steps 54
harbour cruises 19
Hendrix, Jimi 31
Henry Art Gallery 45
Hiram M Chittenden Locks 26
history of Seattle 10–12
hockey 83
horse-racing 83
hostels 86
hotel rate discounts 85
hotels 84–86
houseboats 37
Hurricane Ridge 21
hydro races 83

I

IMAX 29
International District (ID) 41
Internet café 83
itineraries 14–15

J

Japanese Garden 47
jazz 80

K

Kerry Viewpoint 51
Klondike Museum 39

L

LaConner 21
Lake Union 15, 37
Lake View Cemetery 58
Lake Washington Boulevard 56
laser shows 81
Lincoln Park 51
litter 89
lost property 93

M

Madison Park 51, 54
Madison Park
    (neighbourhood) 55
Magnolia Bluff Bike Trail
    56
mail 92
Matthews Beach 51
media and communications
    92–93
medical treatment 93
medicines 93
Metro 91
metropolitan area 9
Microsoft 6, 8
money 89
Monorail 35, 91
Mt Baker 6
Mt Rainier 20
Museum of Flight 43
Museum of History and
    Industry (MOHAI) 52
museums, Eastside 52
music venues 79, 80–81

N

national holidays 89
neighbourhoods 55
newspapers and magazines
    93
Nordic Heritage Museum
    52

O

Occidental Park totems
    53
Odyssey Maritime
    Discovery Center 32, 60
office hours 89
Olympic Mountains 6
Olympic National Park
    21
opening hours 89
opera 79
Out to Lunch Weekday
    Concerts 59
outdoor concerts 79

P

Pacific Science Center 29
parks 50–51
Peace Garden 35
pharmacies 93
Pike Place Market 16, 33
Pioneer Square 17, 39
places of worship 89–90

police 93
population 8, 9
Point Elliott Treaty 12
post offices 92
postal services 92
public toilets 90
public transport 91–92
Puget Sound 26

R

radio 93
REI (Recreational
    Equipment Inc) 40
Royal British Columbia
    Museum 20

S

Sacred Circle Gallery of
    American Indian Art 24
Sculpture Garden 35
Sea-Tac International
    Airport 88
Sealth, Chief 7, 12, 34
seasons 88
Seattle Aquarium 32
Seattle Art Museum (SAM)
    36
Seattle Asian Art Museum
    (SAAM) 42
Seattle Center 35
Seattle Children's Theater
    60
Security Pacific Bank Tower
    54
Seward Park 51
Shilshole Marina 50
shop hours 89
shopping 70–77
shopping districts 70
sightseeing, organised 19
Smith Tower 54
smoking etiquette 8, 89
soccer, indoor 83
Sound Garden 53
Space Needle 30
sport and leisure 56–57, 83
stamps 92
statistical information 9
streetcar 92
Suquamish Museum 34
swimming beaches 51

T

taxis 91
telephones 92–93
television 93
theatre 78

ticket outlets 79, 90
Tillicum Village 19
time differences 90
tipping 89
trains 88
translation services 93
travelling to Seattle 88
twenty-four hour services
    93

U

University District 55
University of Washington
    15, 44

V

Victoria, British Columbia
    20
video arcade 81
visitor information 90
Volunteer Park 42
Volunteer Park Water Tower
    42, 58

W

Waiting for the Interurban
    53
walking tours, guided 19
walks and evening strolls
    16–18
Washington Mutual
    Building 54
Washington Park Aboretum
    47
waterfront 17, 32
weights and measures
    90
West Point lighthouse
    24
Westlake Park 38
Whidbey Island 21
wineries 59
Wing Luke Museum 41,
    52
Woodland Park Zoo 28

Y

Ye Olde Curiosity Shop 32,
    76

CityPack
Seattle

Written by Suzanne Tedesko
Edited, designed and produced by
AA Publishing
Maps © Automobile Association Developments Limited 1999, 2002
City-centre maps on inside front and back covers © Rand McNally 1998, 2002
R.L. #89–S–123
Fold-out map © Rand McNally 1998, 2002 R.L. #89–S–123

Distributed in the United Kingdom by AA Publishing, Millstream, Maidenhead Road, Windsor, Berkshire, SL4 5GD.

The contents of this publication are believed correct at the time of printing. Nevertheless, the publishers cannot be held responsible for any errors or omissions or for changes in the details given in this guide or for the consequences of any reliance on the information provided by the same. Assessments of attractions, hotels, restaurants and so forth are based upon the author's own personal experience and, therefore, descriptions given in this guide necessarily contain an element of subjective opinion which may not reflect the publishers' opinion or dictate a reader's own experiences on another occasion.

We have tried to ensure accuracy in this guide, but things do change and we would be grateful if readers would advise us of any inaccuracies they may encounter.

ISBN 0 7495 3232 7

Published by AA Publishing (a trading name of Automobile Association Developments Limited, whose registered office is Millstream, Maidenhead Road, Windsor, Berkshire, SL4 5GD. Registered number 1878835).

Colour separation by Daylight Colour Art Pte Ltd, Singapore
Printed and bound by Dai Nippon Printing Co (Hong Kong) Ltd.

ACKNOWLEDGEMENTS
The Automobile Association would like to thank the following photographers, libraries and associations for their assistance in the preparation of this book:
The Boeing Company 48a, 48b; Fifth Avenue Theatre 54 (Dick Busher); Frank O. Gehry & Associates Inc. 31a (Joshua White); Museum of Flight 43a, 43b; Rex Features Ltd 31b; Spectrum Colour Library 21; University of Washington 44a; Woodland Park Zoo 28b (Renee De Martin)
All remaining pictures were taken by James Tims and are held in the Association's own library (AA Photo Library) with the exception of the following page: Chris Coe 20.
Cover images: AA Photo Library (James Tims).

The author would like to thank Jalyn Tani and Jerry Waugh for their invaluable assistance.

ORIGINAL COPY-EDITOR *John Mapps*
INDEXER *Marie Lorimer*
REVISION VERIFIER *Suzanne Tedesko, Allison Austin*
COVER DESIGN *Fabrizio La Rocca, Tigist Getachew*
MANAGING EDITOR *Sheila Hawkins*

TITLES IN THE CITYPACK SERIES
• Amsterdam • Bangkok • Barcelona • Beijing • Berlin • Boston • Brussels & Bruges •
• Chicago • Dublin • Florence • Hong Kong • Lisbon • London • Los Angeles • Madrid •
• Melbourne • Miami • Montréal • Munich • New York • Paris • Prague • Rome •
• San Francisco • Seattle • Shanghai • Singapore • Sydney • Tokyo • Toronto • Venice •
• Vienna • Washington •